PRAISE

5 Habits for an Abundant Christian Life

"In all my days...

During my time in the US Marine Corps, over the past 20 years as an entrepreneur and today serving founders, CEOs and executives around America...

...I have never met a man like Glenn Siddle.

From his strong Faith, to his pure humility to his deep love and affection for his wife, daughters and their husbands, Glenn stands out. He also has a deep devotion and love for his work and employees. This is where Glenn is distinguished in my eyes. It is rare to meet a person as successful as Glenn that has learned to keep that "whole life" success in balance. In Christ, Glenn continues to do this and stands as a testimony of God's grace on a person who will trust Him!

As you read this book, you will not only be equipped to live the abundant life that Christ promises but you will also be inspired and filled with faith as you hear the extraordinary work God has done in Glenn and wants to do in and through all of us!"

Phil Nicaud
Founder/CEO - Legendary Leadership Consultants

5 HABITS

FOR AN

ABUNDANT
CHRISTIAN LIFE

Unlocking the Secret for
an Above Average Life

GLENN SIDDLE

5 HABITS FOR AN ABUNDANT CHRISTIAN LIFE

ISBN 978-1-7335083-0-8 (Paperback)
ISBN 978-1-7335083-1-5 (Ebook)

Printed in the United States

Dedication

I dedicate this book to the twenty young men who came to the Oaks Retreat 2018. You guys have given me the passion to put these words on paper.

Table of Contents

Foreword

Do you know people that seem to have it all together? And not the kind of 'having it all together' that's too good to be true. But the kind of success that is genuine, true to life, exemplary, admirable, consistent, virtuous, storm weathering, and passionate. One of those people in my life is Glenn Siddle. I've known Glenn, and his wife Lucy, since serving as the youth pastor to their twin daughters over a decade ago. Watching Glenn navigate life is contagious but can also be perplexing unless you understand how it happens. There's a method to it, a process that's not only proven by the life Glenn lives but just so happens to be straight from the Bible.

The title of this book could've easily been 'Success is No Accident.' But a book with that title might convey the wrong message. You would first need to understand that the ultimate level of success on earth is to live an abundant life. The kind of abundance that Jesus came and died to give us. A life so attractive that others are drawn to it, positively impacting them in ways they don't necessarily understand. To be that person and live that life you must first be willing to *"seek with all your heart" (Jeremiah 29:13)*.

In our society, we look for quick fixes, with guaranteed results, and long-term success. Realistically we know this combination is impossible. We search for the keys to this formula and often hold others accountable when we don't achieve our desired results. You could spend decades reading books and attending seminars in an attempt to find your habits or formulas. But Glenn has done it for you. This book is a 'greatest hits' of leadership and life principles with the Bible as its framework. And Glenn is a living example of the fruits of these habits. So, while this book may not solve all the world's problems, you'll be surprised at how quickly God will reward your obedience with sustainable results when you follow Glenn's roadmap.

I am honored to write the foreword for this book. But in reality, it's a daunting task to try and put into words the influence Glenn Siddle has on my life and lives all around me. If you know him, you understand my challenge. I look up to Glenn as a man of God who doesn't just talk the talk but also walks the walk. He has *"dwelled in the land; he has cultivated faithfulness" (Psalm 37:3)*. He and Lucy have passionately pursued a life of extreme faith, living out what they have learned and seeing God bless it. They are generous in all they do, especially in equipping young leaders for success in their lives, and ultimately the lives of their family, friends, coworkers, neighbors, and community.

So, if you haven't met Glenn, I am excited to introduce him to you. Meet him through the reading of this book, the habits he shares, and the life he lives. His hunger for God is contagious and remains as passionate today as it was over 30 years ago when he started down this path. If you adhere to these simple, biblical principles, you can join Glenn on this journey. You'll begin a positive trajectory towards achieving and sustaining a more abundant life and having an eternal impact.

Mark Pettus, President
Highlands College

Acknowledgments

I want to thank the following people for making this a reality:

Michelle Vandepas, for coaching me through this process. Without you, this would not have happened.

Mark Bowman, for teaching me the critical importance of studying my Bible.

Bob Weiner, for teaching me about faith.

Amanda Watson and Eric Mann, my Vice Presidents at work, for allowing me the time and freedom to write this book. You two are the best!

Phil Nicaud, my Executive Coach, for planting the seed for me to write this book.

Pastor Mark Pettus, for all your encouragement with this project, and for your valued friendship.

My two daughters, Melissa and Melanie, for setting standards in your lives that make me strive to push myself.

And mostly, my sweet wife, Lucy, for always believing in me, being at my side, never settling for the easy road, and being willing to do what God has wanted. You make this journey fun!

Introduction

"I came that they may have life, and
have it abundantly." John 10:10

The purpose of this book is to help any person who
is hungry to achieve more in life. I believe that
God did not put us on this earth to live an average
life, but that He has instilled in each of us gifts that,
if used properly, will enable us to live the abundant
life that Jesus came to give us. This abundant life has
nothing to do with how much money we make or what
amount of material success we attain. What really
matters is whether we are fulfilling our purpose for
which we were created and having a positive impact
on those around us.

One of the best ways to understand this abundant-life
concept is to read the first half of Deuteronomy 28,

where God explains the fruit that will come from an obedient person willing to make certain choices. To summarize in today's terms, think of enjoying every area of your life and having success in it. For instance, enjoying getting up and going to work. Or having your marriage get better with each passing year, and falling more in love each year. Perhaps having children who grow up loving God and becoming contributors to society in meaningful ways. Having great relationships with each of your children. Maybe having the money to help others and pay your bills always on time. Being out of debt completely. This list could go on and on, but you get the point; see success in each and every area of your life. This doesn't mean it ever gets perfect, or that storms don't come, but it is a life that is achievable.

To achieve this abundant life, it will take concerted effort. As each of us look around us, we can tell that not everyone achieves it. Everywhere you look there is stress: divorce, financial struggles, and so on. It does not have to be this way! I am not going to share secrets that are only available to a few, but truths that are there for anyone willing to listen and obey them. When we see the promises in the Bible that are available to us, we can also see that often the promises are results of doing certain things or living our lives in such a way that God will bless us. One of my goals of this book is to uncover some of these truths that I have found and that have worked for me.

I will not apologize for using the Bible as the source of these truths. This Book has changed my life in very tangible ways that I will share with you If that offends you, as is common in today's culture, then maybe this book is not for you. I firmly believe that, with everything in society changing so fast, the Word of God is the one thing that is always the same. In other words, the truths found in it are the same for any generation.

The habits I will share with you are not something someone has passed on to me, but rather habits that I have lived for more than 30 years. I believe these habits have had a profound impact on my life. I found them early in my walk with God when I was desperate to change the life I was living.

Because I know where I came from, as one of four children of immigrant parents with very little going for me, I can honestly say that an abundant life is there for anyone willing to discipline themselves to reach their potential.

"God gave us the gift of life; it is up to us to give ourselves the gift of living well." Voltaire

Preface

My Story

I am constantly in awe of how God has taken such an average kid as me and given me the life I now have. As I reflect on the many blessings in my life, I have come to the realization that it is the habits I have formed over the years and the decisions I have made that have enabled me to be living the life I live today. I often think I do not deserve all that God has done for me, but as I read the Bible, I realize that God truly loves us as a Father. He wants the best for us, which we may achieve if we live by standards He has set. As a father myself, I see how I feel about my kids when I see them making good decisions about their lives. It makes me want to cheer for them in the biggest possible way.

Let me be clear that nothing I will talk about in this book has anything to do with us going to heaven. There is only one way to get there: accepting what Jesus did on the cross to pay for our sins. We cannot work our way to heaven but can only acknowledge and accept what He has already done. I do believe, though, that there are ways to live a better life here on earth if we make certain choices. Jesus said that He came to give us *"life, and life more abundantly" (John 10:10)*. This abundant life is my focus here. There are so many promises in the Bible that explain how our lives can be better if we simply do the things it says. Consider the guidance like a father telling his son to do certain things that will improve his life because the father has more life experiences and wants the best for his son. This is why God gave us the Bible — to steer our lives in a way to get the best out of our time here on earth and impact the greatest amount of people.

There will be stories throughout the book that are personal to me, but I share them so that many of you will relate to my beginnings and my path. I grew up as a very average kid in a very average family. My parents were great people who emigrated from Scotland after World War II. They took us to church every week and even enrolled us in a private Christian high school. But I was so rebellious and so lost that I wanted nothing to do with God. I was neither great in sports nor a good student in school. As a matter of fact, there was nothing that made me rise above the crowd. I say this because I see young people all the time with much more going for them than I had, and I desperately want to see them make the best of this life because we all only get one shot. If God can take an average guy like me and give me the life I now have, He can do it with anyone willing to change. The Bible clearly says that *"God is not one to show partiality" (Acts 10:34)*. I firmly believe this means He will do great things for anyone who is willing to seek Him out.

My journey actually started when I was twenty-two years old, enrolled in college. I was already living wildly when I got to college, and things got much worse while I was there. I was living a life that was taking me nowhere. My older brother wanted me to drop out of college and live the same party lifestyle he did. I could see the destruction that surrounded him and his friends; I knew deep down that if I didn't make a radical change to my life, I would be heading down the same path.

During my first quarter at college, I met a young man who would have a significant impact on me. For four years, he came to my apartment and tried to get me to come to church. He could tell by the way I was living that I was extremely lost, but he did not judge me for it. Rather, he kept after me as a real friend who cared. He was the one person I knew to call when I was desperate. We were both pursuing the same major, and after four years he graduated with honors while I was still technically a sophomore. I knew I needed a change; then came a wakeup call. After four years of heavy partying, I was suspended for six months because my grades were so poor. I was told that if I did come back I would have to maintain a B average, which seemed impossible for me to achieve.

During these six months I worked and partied like nothing had changed. Then, the night before I was moving back to school, I could not sleep. I lay awake all night, thinking where my life was heading and realizing that if I didn't make significant changes, college was not going to work out for me. I wanted more out of life than what the world was offering me at the time and knew something had to happen soon. All I knew to do was to call my buddy who was now working toward a Master's program.

As soon as I arrived in town to start school again, I contacted him, and he invited me to his church. When I went that day, I heard a message I had never heard before that changed me forever. I wanted to believe there was a God, but had never seen anything tangible to convince me. The message that day was meant for me. Maybe it was because I was so ready to change, but I finally believed there was a God who could give me hope to live a life that could make a difference.

When I got back to my apartment, I immediately cleaned out everything that would be a distraction. I won't go into all the details, but there was a lot there that could be a hindrance for me succeeding in this new direction. I felt that I was given one last chance and wanted to make the most of it.

My new Pastor, Mark Bowman, recognized that I needed serious help and he took the time to mentor me. He actually told all the girls in the church to stay away from me because he didn't know yet if I was serious. (I married one of those girls and have had 33 great years together, raising two wonderful daughters. I will talk more on that later.) Mark saw that if I was going to make it, I would need to radically change my lifestyle. I even got rid of my television and my stereo, so I could spend my time on more constructive activities.

As Mark mentored me, he would recommend two or three books to buy and read, and then we would discuss them. I had never read books unless they were required for school. Although reading books is not one of the core habits I am discussing in this book, it has had a profound impact on me and I continue reading positive books to this day.

Over the next year and a half, a foundation was laid in my life that would change me forever. I did graduate with a degree in Mechanical Engineering in one and a half more years and made the best grades I had ever made. More importantly, I got an education in life and how to make decisions that would not just affect me, but also my future wife and future children.

During this time, a Bible verse really grabbed my attention and set me on a journey of discovery. *2 Chronicles 16:9 says, "For the eyes of the Lord move to and fro throughout the earth that He may strongly support those whose heart is completely His."* I was amazed that the God who created everything was actually interested in strongly supporting a man whose heart was His. I couldn't think of anyone I knew whom I could say had this strong support, but I desperately wanted to know what it looked like and was willing to do what it took to get there. It seemed that the answer was to find out what "giving my heart completely to Him" meant, so I started my journey to figure it out.

We can all say we would love to have God's strong support, so please allow me in these next pages to unlock what I have found through focused study regarding this concept. Each habit I discuss comes directly from the Scriptures. I approached this when I was a young man, as a child with simple faith who decided that if I read it in the Bible, I was going to believe it. I would not pick and choose what was true, but would believe it all. Of course, we must put things in context for when it was written, but God chose the stories and words for a reason to help His kids understand more about Him and how to live our lives.

Please understand that this does not mean I am perfect, or anywhere close. Anyone who knows me will tell you that my wife is much closer to a saint than I am. I am just a person like you who wanted to make a difference in this life.

When I finally graduated from college, I worked as an engineer for seven years. I then left the corporate world and became self-employed. Since then, I have started over 20 companies. I presently own seven companies, all of which are successful. I certainly don't say that to brag because I know my roots — and God gets all the credit. I want you to understand that if God can do this for me, He can do it for anyone willing to pay the price.

Let me briefly explain how this book has come about so that you may have some perspective. My twin daughters went to college two hours away from our home. We had spent time during their early years at a lake where we shared a house with my wife's brother. There were many great memories formed over those years of their lives. Because I was self-employed, I quickly learned that, for me to have quality time with my girls, I needed to be away from my home office and computer. I have always loved to work and when I was at home, I would rather be in my office than doing anything else. Because spending time with the girls was an important value of mine, we decided to invest in a lake house.

When college came for them, we made the decision to build our own house, so we could allow them to invite their friends more often. This proved to be a very smart move for our family.

During their four years in college, we hosted dozens upon dozens of college students who would come for the weekend, learn to ski, swim, hang out, eat good food, and have a genuine good time. We got very close to these young people and, over time, formed relationships that allowed us to speak truths into their lives. I think it is fair to say that we became like a second set of parents to many of these great young people.

At the end of four years, we took about twenty of these folks down to the beach to celebrate some of them graduating. I knew it might be the last time this specific group would be together because many of them had jobs in various parts of the country. On one of the last nights I asked them before dinner if I could share with them what I believed it took to be a success in life. They agreed and listened intently as I shared what became the habits that I have put into this book. I shared with them as if it was the final instructions I would give my own children as they went out into the world.

Shortly after this trip, I hired an executive life coach to help me gain focus for the next step in my life. My wife and I had built several successful businesses, raised two wonderful girls who are both now married to amazing young men, and been blessed to see and do a lot of amazing things. But we both realized that we still had a lot to give; we wanted to be intentional with finding the next area where we could have the biggest impact.

During a two-day retreat with this coach, he asked me about what in life I was most passionate. I told him I wanted to help mentor these young men I had been so fortunate to get to know over the past few years at the lake. I saw that there seemed to be many more girls at college seeking God's will for their lives than there were guys. It seemed that most of the guys were more focused on the party scene, as I was at their age. I knew there was a better way to live and I wanted to help them see this.

As I explained this to the coach, he challenged me to consider getting these men together for a weekend re-treat so that I could share with them some of my life lessons. I thought about this and talked it through with my wife and realized it may be a good idea. Because most of these men had now graduated college and were all over the country with their careers, I knew it would be hard to get them in one location. I put together an email and sent it out saying that if they would take a weekend of their time and fly to Alabama, I would cover their expenses and spend a full weekend pouring into them truths that I felt would make them more successful in life. I sent this email to twenty-two young guys expecting to get maybe six to eight to respond. To my surprise, all responded and twenty out of twenty-two came. To say I was surprised by this group's response would be an understatement!

I organized the weekend and invited two pastors and my executive coach to speak to these guys over a three-day period. I was going to speak on Saturday night, and as I was thinking about what to share. It occurred to me that the habits I had been sharing with them over the years were what they needed to hear put together in one message. I shared with them real-life stories as if they were all my sons. I wanted them to succeed in life. The response I received as we wrapped up was incredible.

These habits can change anyone's life who will discipline themselves and follow them. Many will say this isn't for them, and that is fine. I am confident though that there is someone out there like I was, who was hungry to just be told what to do and will go and do it. That one person could go and change the world for the better!

Let's begin our journey with what I believe is the most important habit you can have in your life.

Habit Number One
Read the Bible

"This book of the law shall not depart from your mouth, but you shall meditate on it day and night, so that you may be careful to do according to all that is written in it; for then you will make your way prosperous, and then you will have success." Joshua 1:8

Our ultimate goal in our Christian walk should be to hear the words "Well done, good and faithful servant. Enter into My rest." Our salvation is secured when we accept what Jesus did on the cross for us and decide to live for Him. Jesus told the criminal hanging on the cross next to Him that he would see Jesus in heaven because he believed that Jesus was the Son of

God. This book is not written to help explain salvation, but to share some insight into how we can live a more abundant life on earth and have as big an impact as possible. Our goal should not be to just barely get into heaven, but to have such an impact on this earth that when we get there, people will be celebrating because of how we lived our lives.

Jesus said that He chose us out of the world to bear fruit. This tells me that my responsibility as a Christian is to use my talents and abilities to help others. God has given all of us different gifts, and our job is to recognize them and use them for His purpose. The Bible says that people have different responses to hearing the Word. Some simply reject it; some let the worries of the world choke it out; but some receive it and then go and bear fruit, *"thirty, sixty, and one hundred-fold" (Matthew 13:23)*. Let's be the person that lives a life to have one hundred-fold returns!

To accomplish this return, we should seek the truths that are in the Bible on how we should live our lives. I will begin our journey together with one of my life verses:

> *"This book of the law shall not depart from your mouth, but you shall meditate on it day and night, so that you may be careful to do according to all that is written in it; for then you will make your*

*way prosperous, and then you'll have
success" (Joshua 1:8).*

This verse had a significant impact on me when I read
it for the first time in college. I decided then that I
would make a habit every day to read and meditate
on the Word, so I could be "careful to do what was in
it." I mentioned being mentored by my pastor during
these first few months of my new life. One thing he
always asked when I went in to speak with him was
whether I had been in the Word that day. If I said no,
he would tell me to come back when I had spent time
in it. He was simply trying to teach me the principle
of the importance of the Word.

Remember I was desperate for a change in my life and
was willing to do anything to figure out how to improve my odds. When I made my decision to change
my life and live for the Lord, it was radical. I knew the
life of drugs and partying was not the answer for me.
I knew I needed to change my habits and that the best
place for me to look was in the Bible. I took the time
I had been spending on partying and instead went to
the library to study for school; a habit I had not de-
veloped up until then. I also spent much time reading
my Bible. For that first year I averaged between one
and two hours of reading my Bible per day. This may
sound like a lot, but I had plenty of time because my
bad habits were gone. I told all my "friends" what I
had done, and they all quit coming to my apartment.

They wanted nothing to do with this change I had made, so it worked out well to free up my time!

When I read Joshua 1:8 during these early years, I saw God offering a blueprint for Joshua to follow to have success in his life. I felt that if it was good enough for Joshua, it was good enough for me. God spoke this verse to Joshua when he was about to lead Israel into the Promised Land, after the Israelites had spent years wandering through the wilderness. Moses had passed away. Joshua was now leading the Israelites, and he was nervous. I know this because three times in the first chapter of the book of Joshua, God said to be "strong and courageous." I don't believe He would have said this three times if Joshua was full of confidence! The blueprint was the book of the law that Moses had left for Joshua, which is presently what we know as the first five books of the Bible. This was instruction for how the Israelites were to live their lives.

Similarly, several hundred years later, the psalmist said:

> *"How blessed is the man who does not walk in the counsel of the wicked, nor stand in the path of sinners, nor sit in the seat of scoffers! But his delight is in the law of the Lord, and in His law, he meditates day and night. And he will be like a tree firmly planted by streams of*

> *water, which yields its fruit in its sea-*
> *son, and its leaf does not wither; and in*
> *whatever he does, he prospers" (Psalms*
> *1:1-3).*

Notice the similarity to the verse in Joshua. If we meditate on God's Word day and night, we will find success!

These two passages in Joshua and Psalms both use the word "meditate." When we read, we are not merely trying to turn the pages, but are taking time to think about what we are reading. We consider what God is trying to say to His people— to us. We meditate on what we are reading and should be asking God to reveal to us how this relates to our life, and how we should apply it to our situation. Having simple faith that God wants us to know Him allows the Word to come alive in our lives and become real to us. What a great thought it is to have a loving Father who would put in writing what we should do to get the most out of this life!

John told us in the first chapter of his book that *"Jesus was the Word of God, that He became flesh and dwelt among us" (John 1:14).* What better way for God to show us His love than to send Jesus in the form of a man— Someone we could both relate to and learn from? Jesus's incarnation allows us to understand more about how we are to live our lives, but we must make the commitment to seek the truths that He offers.

An important point here is that Jesus is the *"same yesterday, today, and forever" (Hebrews 13:8)*. If Jesus is the Word of God that became flesh and dwelt among us, and He is the same yesterday, today, and forever, then it stands to reason that the Word of God is the same yesterday, today, and forever. This means that what was written by Moses over four thousand years ago still applies today. What was written by David three thousand years ago applies today. What was written by the prophets and by the apostles still applies today.

Obviously, the cultures have changed dramatically since the times when the Bible was written. As we read it with an open mind, understanding the context of the times when it was written, we can extract the truths that God wants us to see today. We can see that the Bible is relevant to today's culture.

I believe the Bible's relevance is God's way of leading us into a deeper relationship with Him. Throughout this book I will share personal stories of when this has happened in my life, to show how God has used His Word to become real to me.

When I first became serious about reading the Bible, my older brother loved to debate with me and tell me how many contradictions it had. The problem was that he had never read it in full but was simply repeating what he had heard others say. After reading it completely through at least twenty times, I can say that it does make complete sense when you read it in its entirety, holding everything in proper context.

A good example would be the sacrifices in the Old Testament. If you are supposed to read everything literally without considering context, then you must perform all the sacrifices commanded in the first five books of Moses! However, when you read the New Testament, you see how Jesus came to take the place of those sacrifices and became the final sacrifice for our sins.

Many of the stories in the Old Testament focused on Israel in the time before Christ. Although this was written specifically for the times in which they were living, we can still learn from history so that we don't repeat the mistakes that the Israelites made. Israel was often in war, and the temple that Solomon built in Jerusalem was destroyed because of the people's rebellion from God. We can learn from these stories that there are consequences here on earth for our actions, and that if we turn from God and disobey Him, we will suffer for it. This doesn't mean He doesn't love us, but He expects us to live a certain way if we want to live the abundant life.

Of course, some of the Prophets, like Ezekiel and Daniel, spoke about future times that have still not taken place, so it is important to understand them also.

The entire Bible, regardless of the chapter's author, is the *"inspired Word of God" (2 Timothy 3:16)*. If we approach it as a living document that God sent to us to help us live our lives, we can receive instruction and direction for our lives. (There will be more on that in the next chapter.)

Jesus told us that *"Man shall not live on bread alone, but on every word that proceeds out of the mouth of God" (Matthew 4:4)*. He made the point that understanding the words that come from God are as important as bread itself. In other words, we should look at our study of the Scriptures as important as eating every day. We would not last long without food; we must look at getting our spiritual food just as often.

So how should we study and read our Bible? I don't believe there is one method that works for everyone but having the hunger for it and seeing it as necessary food for living will help us develop a love for it. We always tend to find time for the things we love. By reading on a regular basis and seeing all the promises that are in the Bible, we develop the passion. With the access to the Internet today, you can download many options for reading. There are one-year Bible readings where you read a passage from both the Old and New Testaments daily, plus a Psalm and a Proverb. This works for many Christians and will enable you to get through the Bible in one year. There are also chronological Bibles that put the books in the order they were written. This is helpful to keep history in perspective.

My preferred reading technique is simply to read from start to finish each year. This takes between fifteen and twenty minutes per day. I like to do it in the morning before I start my day, but that hasn't always worked out. Being self-employed, I've had many days when I had to hit the ground running when I woke up in the morning. The key to being successful with this is to find what works for you and to not allow yourself to get under any condemnation if it doesn't work out every day.

The advantage to reading the One Year Bible is that if you miss a day, you can just pick up on the next day and keep going. The purpose of doing this is not to check a goal off your list, but rather to gain the knowledge and understanding of how we are to live our lives.

I am also a big fan of highlighting in my Bible. I write in the margins and use a highlighter for verses that mean something to me. Maybe they are promises from God for encouragement, or just instructions on how to live. It is nice to be able to just turn pages to find highlighted areas for encouragement. I have also enjoyed gathering verses together on common topics, like faith, boldness, prosperity, etc. and then writing them together to see the common themes. This helps to gain a better understanding of what God is wanting us to know.

The key to being successful at reading your Bible is to keep doing it until it becomes a habit. There are studies that show it takes twenty-one days of repeating an activity for it to become a habit. Other studies show that it takes longer; the main thing is to keep doing it until it becomes a passion, until you don't want to let a day go by without spending a little time with your Bible. For me, it is a time I look forward to every day because I feel I get instruction and inspiration on how to live my life. The Bible is also so full of promises for the life we can have if we search for them diligently. I believe that God is pleased when He sees us eager to learn more about Him.

As we are spending time in the Bible, it is important to know that it isn't just another book. Remember that *"all Scripture is inspired by God,"* which means that God had His hand in the entire Book *(2 Timothy 3:16)*. Paul also told the Thessalonians, *"We constantly thank God that when you received from us the word of God's message, you accepted it not as the word of men, but for what it really is, the word of God, which also performs*

*its work in you who believe" (1 Thessalonians 2:13).
"The word of God is alive and active. Sharper than any
double-edged sword, it penetrates even to dividing soul
and spirit, joints and marrow; it judges the thoughts and
attitudes of the heart" (Hebrews 4:12).* So, as we read,
we should treat the Bible like it is God Himself actually speaking to us.

Two of my favorite books in the Bible are the two
books Paul wrote to Timothy. I love them because it is
like a father speaking to his son. Paul was Timothy's
mentor and teacher. Early in my Christian life, I
wanted to be a Timothy who sat at the feet of a Paul,
someone who could teach me everything about God.
Now I am at a place in my life where I can be a Paul
to many Timothys.

Paul was radically transformed while he was persecuting Christians. After Jesus had been crucified and had
risen from the dead, He appeared to Paul. Subsequent
to His appearance, Paul was on his way to Damascus
when he was blinded by a light and heard a voice asking him why he was persecuting Jesus. The people
with Paul heard the voice but could see nothing. This
encounter with Jesus so changed Paul that he gave
the rest of his life teaching people about this Jesus
whom he now believed was the Son of God. His many
letters, including the letters to Timothy, have given
Christians encouragement and instruction on how to
live for almost two thousand years now.

11

Timothy was like a son to Paul and had traveled with him to set up churches. Timothy was young and was left in charge of a growing church at Ephesus, so Paul wrote to encourage Timothy for the big task in front of him. One of Paul's admonishments to Timothy was, *"Be diligent to present yourself approved to God as a workman who does not need to be ashamed, handling accurately the word of truth" (2 Timothy 2:15)*. Paul was encouraging Timothy to stay focused on the truths of Who Jesus was and what He came to do on this earth. At the time Paul wrote this, the Bible was not yet one collective book, so he was telling Timothy to read and study the letters that were written about Jesus. I believe that if Paul were writing this today, he would be telling Timothy to study his Bible— and especially the Gospels— diligently every day.

Let's now explore several of the benefits that go along with studying our Bible and living a life that pleases God.

Benefits of Reading the Word

❖ We can know God

Our primary focus for reading the Bible should be to get to know God - His attributes, His characteristics, and His promises. If we truly believe that He is the

God who created us and formed us in our mother's womb, then He knows more about us than we know about ourselves. We should, in turn, be diligent to get to know Him.

In Matthew 7, Jesus told the religious leaders of the day that only those who knew God would enter the kingdom of heaven. They were trying to reason with Him that their religious acts were making them righteous, but Jesus brought the focus back to actually having a relationship with God. It is amazing to think that God actually does want a relationship with us here on earth. The Bible says He knows every hair on our head, so it seems that to have a healthy relationship we need to do our part to get to know Him.

The Old Testament says that if we are boastful about anything, it should be about knowing God. *Jeremiah 9:24, NIV* says, *"'But let him who boasts boast in this, that he understands and knows me, that I am the Lord who practices steadfast love, justice, and righteousness in the earth. For in these things I delight,' declares the Lord."* This is just one of many verses that says we can get to know Him and learn about the many promises that are there for us. The best way for us to do this is to study the Book that He gave us.

People who know me know that I love my children immensely, as many other parents do. I always want the best for them. But I can see in the Bible that God loves me even more than I love my children. He always wants the best for me also. In Matthew it says that, *"If you know how to give good gifts to your children, how much more shall your Father in heaven give what is good to those who ask Him!" (Matthew 7:11)*. Talk about a great promise!

❖ We can find God's will for our lives

One of the biggest questions that young people want to know is how to find out God's will for their lives — where to work, who to marry, where to live, and so forth. I will explore this further in the next chapter on practical ways to hear God's will for your lives, but it also ties in with keeping our mind in the Word. Remember the two passages in Joshua and Psalm 1? Both passages encourage us to meditate on the Word.

Paul wrote in his letter to the Roman church that we could prove the will of God by renewing our mind. The letter says, *"And do not be conformed to this world, but be transformed by the renewing of your mind, that you may prove what the will of God is, that which is good and acceptable and perfect" (Romans 12:2)*.

I believe this verse goes hand in hand with another passage Paul wrote to the church in Ephesus. There Paul wrote, *"Husbands, love your wives, just as Christ also loved the church and gave Himself up for her; that*

He might sanctify her, having cleansed her by the washing of water with the word; that He might present to Himself the church in all her glory, having no spot or wrinkle or any such thing; but that she should be holy and blameless" (Ephesians 5:25-27).

Paul said husbands should love their wives as Christ loved the church. He then explained that Jesus cleansed the church and sanctified her with "washing of water with the word." In other words, Jesus was teaching the church how to live a godly life by speaking the words that He came to give. When I read these passages as a young Christian in my twenties, I believed that I could renew my mind by studying the words that Jesus gave us and therefore understanding what God's will was in my life. Again, we will explore this more in the next chapter on hearing from God but meditate on that thought for a minute and consider how it can help you.

❖ We will keep our lives pure

Isaiah 59:2 tells us that our sin separates us from God. None of us can live a perfect life, but when we are continuing a life of sin it makes it difficult for God to answer our prayers. Therefore, it is important to keep our lives pure.

Thankfully, as often is the case, the Bible has the answer for keeping our lives pure. *"How can a young man keep his way pure? By keeping it according to Thy word. With all my heart I have sought Thee; do not let me wander from Thy commandments. Thy word I have treasured in my heart, that I may not sin against Thee"* (Psalm 119:9-11). We see here that to keep our lives pure, we simply live our lives in such a way that lines up with the Bible. The only way to do this is to study the Bible with this purpose.

❖ We will find favor in His sight

As I mentioned in the beginning of the book, one of the Scriptures I read as a new believer in college that really impacted me was *2 Chronicles 16:9: "God searches for a man whose heart is His so that He can strongly support him."* What an amazing concept, that God actually desires to strongly support us! Another way to look at this is that we can gain God's favor. David said in *Psalm 5:12* that *"God will surround the righteous man with favor as with a shield."* David had a heart after God and certainly knew what this favor looked like because he saw God do so many miraculous things in David's life when Saul was trying to kill him.

Moses asked for God's favor as well, and we see that he certainly had it when we read his story. Moses asked, *"Let me know Thy ways, that I may know Thee, so that*

I may find favor in Thy sight" (Exodus 33:13). Moses wanted to know God so that he could have this favor. With all the miracles recorded about Moses' life, as well as the fact that God spoke to him and gave him the Ten Commandments, it is easy to see that he had God's favor.

God also told Moses that if he would be diligent to obey God's word, he would have favor with the nations of the world. *"Now it shall be, if you will diligently obey the Lord your God, being careful to do all His commandments which I command you today, the Lord your God will set you above all the nations of the earth" (Deuteronomy 28:1).* I believe this promise was not just to Moses or just for the people of Israel, but all of us as well. (We will explore in more detail how this promise is the same promise that God had already made to Abraham that He would bless him and multiply him.) In the New Testament, in both Galatians and Hebrews, we are told that this promise is for all believers.

We can also see by the prophet Isaiah that if we revere God's Word and treat it with the respect it deserves, that He will look upon us with favor. *"But this is the one on whom I will look: he who is humble and contrite in spirit and trembles at my word" (Isaiah 66:2).*

As I put these verses together, I see that by keeping a focus on God's Word, the Bible, and adhering to what it says, we can truly have God's favor and have Him answer our prayers. We will explore this more in the next chapter, as getting answers to our prayers is a common question for most Christians.

❖ Our days on earth will be lengthened

None of us knows the number of days we will live on this earth. We can exercise regularly, take vitamins, and eat a healthy diet, but the reality is that we cannot determine how long we will live. That doesn't stop most of us from exercising and eating healthy; we want to do all we can to put ourselves in position to live a long life. The Bible says we can also increase our number of days on this earth by teaching God's Word to our children:

> *"You shall therefore impress these words of Mine on your heart and on your soul and you shall bind them as a sign on your hand, and they shall be as frontals on your forehead. And you shall teach them to your sons, talking of them when you sit in your house and when you walk along the road and when you lie down and when you rise up. And you shall write them on the doorpost of your house and on your gates, so that your days and the days of your sons may be*

> *multiplied on the land which the Lord*
> *swore to your fathers to give them, as*
> *long as the heavens remain above the*
> *earth" (Deuteronomy 11:18-21).*

In *Psalm 91,* one of the greatest psalms, David said that if we *"dwell in the shelter of the Most High,"* many *promises follow, including that "we will be satisfied with a long life, and behold God's salvation."* Again, we cannot determine the length of our days, but anything we can do to help extend them should be a priority so that we can make more of a difference on this earth.

My children will tell you that I was always intentional about teaching them the truths I read in the Bible. I knew that it was my responsibility to teach them and tell them the stories of how God had answered prayers and moved in my life, so when they grew up, they could decide for themselves if that was the life they wanted. I am so thankful to say that they are married and serving God with their husbands today, which is the biggest blessing in my life.

❖ We will be equipped for life

Would you love to be in a position where you are prepared for anything that comes up during your day? The Bible says this is possible. If we are keeping our lives according to the Word, then we can have the promise that Paul gave to Timothy: *"All Scripture is inspired by God and profitable for teaching, for reproof, for correction, for training in righteousness; that the man of God may be adequate, equipped for every good work" (2 Timothy 3:16-17)*.

As we read, study, and meditate on the Scriptures, and live our lives according to what they says, they will teach us, correct us, and train us for every good work. This just gives another reason to form the habit of studying the Word: to be prepared for any good work.

❖ We can have success and bear fruit

It is hard to study the Bible at any length without noticing all the promises of God where He wants us to have success and bear fruit. But it is important to understand that the success God wants for us is linked to having an impact on building His kingdom on this earth and fulfilling His purposes. I will explore this more in Chapter 4, but we cannot ignore the many promises God makes for those who seek Him.

God says that if we seek Him, we shall not be in lack of any good thing. Talk about an amazing promise! *"O fear the Lord, you his saints; for to those who fear Him, there is no want. The young lions do lack and suffer hunger; but they who seek the Lord shall not be in want of any good thing" (Psalm 34:9-10).* This sounds like the abundant life Jesus spoke of, around one thousand years after this Psalm was written. But it is predicated on us seeking God earnestly.

Jesus often spoke in parables, or stories, and He explained that when people hear the Word, there are different responses they will have as to how they receive it. Some will immediately reject it. Others will receive it for a short period and then let people steal it from them, like crabs in a bucket.

The way you keep a crab in a bucket is to put a couple more in there and they will not let any out without pulling them back into the bucket. This sounds like friends and family members who don't want to see you get ahead of them.

But then there is the last group, which hears the Word and accepts it. *"And those are the ones on whom seed was sown on the good soil; and they hear the word and accept it, and bear fruit, thirty, sixty, and a hundredfold" (Mark 4:20).* It should be a goal of each of us to bear as much fruit in this life as possible, because this pleases God.

❖ It helps us defeat the enemy

The Bible is clear that spiritual forces are always at work to wreck our lives. You may call this force the devil, or the enemy, or generally a spiritual force of darkness. The Bible uses all these terms. But what is important is to identify that he is real and will work hard to make our lives miserable. Because of this, we need to focus on preparing for our ministry. Jesus spent thirty years working and preparing for three years of ministry. I believe the devil knew exactly who Jesus was and tried hard to keep Him from fulfilling his earthly purpose. Jesus went into the wilderness and fasted for forty days to prepare Himself. During this period, the devil tempted Him three separate times by offering Jesus wealth and otherwise using deceit to stop Him from what was about to happen. Each time He was tempted, Jesus quoted Scriptures from the Old Testament to counter what the devil was doing.

Paul also exhorts us in Ephesians to resist the devil. When we have problems in our lives, Paul instructs us to put on the armor of God, including the *"sword of the Spirit, which is the word of God" (Ephesians 6:17)*. A sword is used in battle, so we are told to fight our battles against "spiritual forces" with the Word. If we are sick, or depressed, or have lost our job, we should use the Word to fight. It gives us the power over our enemy, which is not flesh and blood.

We have discussed the importance of staying in the Word and making it a vital part of our lives. But just reading the Word is not enough. We must read it with the intention to do what it says. Jesus' brother himself said, *"Prove yourselves doers of the Word, and not merely hearers who delude themselves" (James 1:22)*. To continue on our growth process, we must learn how to live our lives in a manner that pleases God.

In this chapter, we have seen that major benefits come from forming the habit of reading and meditating on the Word; we will know God and see what His will is for our lives. I often speak with young people who are trying to figure out what God wants them to do in a certain situation. I believe it starts with spending time in the Word. God says that if we seek first His kingdom, all things will be added to us. Making Him the major priority in our lives will help every other area work out.

The next chapter will explain how we can hear from God and obey Him. This ties in directly with studying the Word because it is the primary way God speaks to us.

2

Habit Number Two
Learn to Hear and Obey God

"And in your seed all the nations of the earth shall be blessed, because you have obeyed My voice." Genesis 22:18

We achieve the truly abundant Christian life only when we habitually obey God's voice. For this to happen, we must first learn to hear His voice so that we can obey. God has a plan for our lives that can take many different directions, simply because we have decisions to make every day. I believe that the key to obedience in the midst of these decisions is to have an open heart. When our heart is open to pleasing Him and obeying Him, then we can begin to understand His plan for our lives.

Doesn't it make sense that if God is real, He would provide a way to speak to His kids so they can accomplish the purpose for which He put them on earth? God could have easily just created robots that would do what He wanted. But He has laid out a plan through the Bible and provided the Holy Spirit for us to understand our purpose on the earth at the exact time we were put here.

If you are truly listening to Him, He will gently tell you the things you need to do and the directions you need to take. The question is, how do we hear His voice so we can obey? This is a quality that develops as you mature as a Christian. I call it a habit because I believe that, as we practice hearing God and obeying Him with faith, it becomes easier to distinguish when He is talking.

When I go on a trip- whether for a couple of days or several weeks I take my Bible with me. Because I have formed the habit of reading my Bible, it is hard for me to go more than a few days without reading it. It may seem weird to you too, for instance, be sitting in an airport reading a Bible, but it will surprise you how natural it becomes. I guess some people who see me assume I must be a pastor or something, but I am simply trying to get my nourishment for the day!

Remember the woman at the well whom Jesus asked to give Him some water? It wasn't acceptable in their culture for her to be talking to Jesus, but as they talked Jesus told her things about her life that led her to assume He was a prophet. Jesus told her that if she understood who He was, she could receive from Him a living water that would keep her from ever thirsting again. He was saying that having a revelation of who Jesus was would be better than any food or water she could receive. This is how we should approach our study of the Bible, as living water from God.

What does it mean that the Bible is living? It means that it can speak to us in today's terms if we are reading and expecting for God to speak to us through it. Let me give an example.

On a recent trip back from visiting one of my daughters, I was reading the small book of Amos while waiting to board the plane. I was working on this chapter on how to hear God. One verse stood out to me; it says that God shows us His thoughts. What a perfect way to start this chapter, realizing that God will reveal His thoughts to us. *"For behold, He who forms mountains and creates the winds and <u>declares to man what are His thoughts</u>, He who makes dawn into darkness and treads on the high places of earth, the Lord God of hosts is His name"* (*Amos 4:13*, emphasis mine).

So how does God reveal His thoughts to men? Can we really hear His voice and know His will? The answer is absolutely, "Yes!"

The Bible says that without faith it is impossible to please God because we must believe that He is, and that He is a rewarder of those who seek Him (Hebrews 11:6). If we are going to please Him, then we must believe that He exists. To believe that He exists, then we need to believe His Word.

When Jesus told His disciples He was about to be taken from them, they did not understand it. He told them it would be better for them because He was going to send the Holy Spirit, who would be with them always. Jesus had just spent three years pouring His life into His disciples, but told them it would be even better to have the Holy Spirit inside them because He would teach and guide them through life. *"But the Helper, the Holy Spirit, whom the Father will send in My name, He will teach you all things, and bring to your remembrance all that I said to you" (John 14:26).*

The disciples had seen Jesus do many miracles and could not imagine not having Him around to continue what He had started. He was only thirty-three years old and seemed to have so much more time to continue His phenomenal work. But God's plan all along was to impart a Helper to the disciples and let them continue the ministry. By sending the Holy Spirit to live within them, God provided them with a constant Guide who would steer them in what to say and do.

This promise was fulfilled in the book of Acts when the Holy Spirit was poured out on the believers. It is also a promise that we still have today as believers. The Holy Spirit lives inside of us when we get born again.

Remember, it takes faith to please God. Although the concept of having a Holy Spirit live inside us may seem hard to fathom, believe God at His Word and use faith to allow God to guide your life. We may call it our conscience, but all of us have an inner voice that will tell us right from wrong. When we practice listening to this inner voice, we can see that God will speak through it to help us with decisions we have. God knows the future and He wants the best for us as His kids, so as we listen to this voice, we will get direction.

If the Holy Spirit was sent by God to live inside us and direct our paths, then it makes sense that this would be the primary way for God to speak to us. I look at it like this: when I read the Bible, I ask God to reveal truths to me. Sometimes I read something, and I feel a nudge saying to me it is for me. Call it intuition, or an inner feeling, but I believe it is the Holy Spirit bringing something to light in my life He wants me to know.

Hearing from God started right when I became a Christian. I had not been in church for many years but had been in a denominational church as a child and was never told that Christians can hear God's voice. This changed for me quickly when I became a Christian. I didn't have to fully understand the Bible yet to know what I was doing was wrong. I had been using drugs every day for eight years. So immediately, everything in my apartment that I felt would hold me back went in the trash! This may seem radical to you, and nobody was telling me to do it; I just needed a complete culture change if this was going to work for me, and I was so desperate for it to work that I took these radical steps.

For the week following that purge, I felt like a free man. There was just one more area of my life where I wasn't sure what step to take. I had been in a relationship with a girl for two years, and although we didn't talk about marriage, it looked like we were headed that way. Our parents assumed as much because we were together a lot, even though she was in college at another school. Even though she was not a Christian yet, she was on board with getting saved and going into the ministry, if that was what I chose to do. Something just didn't seem right about it. I sat down with my pastor, Mark Bowman, to ask his advice, and he shared with me in very simple terms how I could know God's will for this important decision.

Mark could tell that my heart was pure and that I wanted to do the right thing. After listening to me for a few minutes he said this: "Glenn, forget for a moment what you want to do. Forget what she wants to do. Forget what your mom and dad think you should do and what her mom and dad think you should do. In your heart, what do you think God wants you to do?" So simple and so easy! Mark just told me to clear all my thoughts on what everybody wanted and think about what God wanted. Without hesitation, I said that I believed God wanted me to break up with her.

Then Mark gave me the first Scripture I would ever memorize. He said, *"Trust in the Lord with all your heart, and do not lean on your own understanding. In all your ways acknowledge Him, and He will make your paths straight" (Proverbs 3:5-6).* Mark told me that I did not need to understand it yet, but rather to simply trust God; if I chose what He wanted, He would work it out.

That was the first time I could say that I felt that God was telling me to do something, and I was going to just obey it with faith. That weekend, just days after getting saved, I went to her home and broke up with her. I wouldn't say it was easy, but I knew it was the right thing to do. And as I drove away from her house, it was like the biggest burden had been lifted from me. But the story doesn't end there.

For the next two weeks, I continued to have thoughts about her and our relationship. I wanted them to be gone because I knew I was doing the right thing. I was praying earnestly every day for God to remove all the thoughts I was having. Then, two weeks later, I was standing outside the church on the front lawn with a group of people and I heard a sweet voice say something behind me. A voice inside of me said, "That is going to be your wife!" I turned around and looked at who was speaking and saw this beautiful young lady and my first thought was, "Well, glory to God!"

I did not even know this girl's name; all I knew was that she was usually up front in church on the worship team. I was certainly not looking for a girlfriend and definitely not looking for a wife! But I was so convinced that God had spoken this to me that I went home to my apartment and carved the date on my wooden desk. I knew that one day I would be showing this to her.

For the next year and a half, we spent time together in groups but never dated. I was on probation in school and needed to work hard with no distractions. But a group of us studied together and we got to know each other well. When I was nearing graduation, we went on our first date and I asked her to marry me. She had no clue this was coming, but God had been working on her heart also and she accepted! As I am writing this book, we are celebrating thirty-three years of marriage. We have raised two beautiful daughters who love the Lord and are both married to young men who love the Lord. Our family is very blessed, but I submit to you that it all started because I heard God's voice and was willing to obey. I believe that we could have both married someone else and lived a good life and gone to heaven, but it would not have been God's best for either of us.

Why do I think God spoke to me in front of that church that day? I believe it is because God saw my heart and that I really wanted to do the right thing- whatever would please Him. He didn't want me tormented with impure thoughts. Again, I was not looking for a wife, but I was just looking to please God. And from that day on that lawn I never had those thoughts again about the other girl.

If you ask me how I know that God is real and that He loves me, I can mention many things. But I can just point to the fact that he gave me Lucy as a wife, who is more than I could have ever imagined a wife could be. I can honestly say that we are more in love today than we have ever been, and that each year of our marriage has gotten better than the previous year. I believe this is God's plan when we live an obedient life.

When I talk to young people, one of the biggest questions they have is which person they will marry. My response is that if they will put all of their focus and energy on pleasing God and getting to know *Him*, He will reveal the right person in the right time.

This also happened for both of our girls. Neither of them dated anyone through high school or college. Not because they weren't allowed to, but because they were more focused on pleasing God. Each of their current husbands was their first and last person to date. I see this working in many young marriages that put God first. There are many Scriptures that give promises about our children being blessed when we are obedient, and I can say it is probably the biggest blessing in my life, seeing my children thrive and serving God with their husbands.

If you go back and look at the promise in Deuteronomy 28, part of the blessing includes our offspring (Deuteronomy 28:11). This promise is given to us if we are diligent to obey the Lord. This is a part of an abundant life.

Many well-meaning Christians will tell you that God does not speak today - that this was only for the Bible times. I respectfully disagree. Jesus said that his sheep hear His voice (John 10:27). *Hebrews 11:6* says, *"without faith, it is impossible to please God, for he who comes to God must believe that He is, and that He is a rewarder of those who seek Him."* Rewards come to the person who will seek God earnestly and believe His Word as it is written. It does take faith for us to believe that God will speak to us, so let's keep an open mind and we will see that this is not as hard as it may appear.

Let me further explain how this has worked about for me. When I graduated college, I got my first engineering job at a large textile company with mills throughout the southeast. Each day at lunch, the managers would take an hour and go to local restaurants to eat. I had been a Christian for two years and was so hungry for the Word. Instead of going to eat with everyone, I would drive my truck to a cul-de-sac and get in the back, inside my camper shell, and read my Bible. I didn't care what others thought because I was learning about God and wanted His will for my life.

During this time, I came upon 3 John 2, which says, "Beloved, I pray above all respects that you may prosper and be in good health, as your soul prospers." What an amazing prayer from John! He wanted everyone to prosper and be in good health, which I think we can all say we want. But I was more intrigued by the second part of this verse, "as your soul prospers." I wanted to know what this meant and what it looked like. I had a Bible concordance that takes any word in the Bible and shows every verse it is used in. I started looking at every verse that contained 'soul' and 'prosperity'. I wanted to see how these words tied together and what exactly "soul prosperity" looked like. This led me to an incredible revelation about God that has impacted my life in amazing ways.

The revelation I received is that God does want us to prosper and has a plan for us to achieve it, but it is not so we can have abundance for our own good. God's purpose is for us to use our prosperity to fulfill His purpose on this earth. I will explain this using Abraham's life story.

Abraham is one of the key figures in the Bible and is the father to three world religions. Through his son Isaac come both the Jewish faith and the Christian faith, and through his son Ishmael comes the Islamic faith. Yet Abraham had no children until he was well advanced in years. God promised him around eighty years of age that He was going to give him a son; that the descendants of his son would be great; and that they would inherit the land. Because Sarah was advanced in years, she gave her maid, Hagar, to Abraham assuming that this was the best way to fulfill the promise. Hagar bore Ishmael when Abraham was eighty-six years old, which eventually caused Sarah to be jealous of Hagar and her son. But God had a different plan for Sarah and Abraham.

When Ishmael was thirteen and Abraham was ninety-nine years old, an angel appeared to Abraham and told him that God was going to give him another son through his wife Sarah. Sarah laughed about this because she was beyond childbearing years. She was ninety years old! But God told Abraham, *"nothing is too difficult for the Lord" (Genesis 18:14)*. He also told Abraham that He would establish a covenant with Abraham through his son Isaac. One year later, Sarah bore a son and named him Isaac. This is where the story gets interesting.

Abraham has been told by God that he would have this son in his old age and that there would be descendants proceeding from Isaac who could not even be numbered. When Isaac became a teenager, God did something dramatic to test Abraham's obedience. He told him to sacrifice this son he was promised. Abraham had seen God do a miracle by giving him a son in his old age; and then God tells him to offer this miracle-son as a sacrifice! God was not looking for Abraham to give up his son whom he loved, but was wanting to make sure he would be obedient and trust God. Here is the story as written in Genesis:

> *"Now it came about after these things, that God tested Abraham, and said to him, 'Abraham!' And he said, 'Here I am.' And He said, 'Take now your son, your only son, whom you love, Isaac, and go to the land of Moriah; and offer him there as a burnt offering on one of the mountains of which I will tell you.' So Abraham rose early in the morning and saddled his donkey, and took two of his young men with him and Isaac his son; and he split wood for the burnt offering, and arose and went to the place of which God had told him. On the third*

day Abraham raised his eyes and saw
the place from a distance. And Abraham
said to his young man, 'Stay here with
the donkey, and I and the lad will go
yonder; and we will worship and return
to you.' And Abraham took the wood of
the burnt offering and laid it on Isaac
his son, and he took in his hand the fire
and the knife. So the two of them walked
on together. And Isaac spoke to Abraham
his father and said, 'My father!' And he
said, 'Here I am, my son.' And he said,
'Behold, the fire and the wood, but where
is the lamb for the burnt offering?' And
Abraham said, 'God will provide for
Himself the lamb for the burnt offering,
my son.' So the two of them walked on
together.

"Then they came to the place of which
God had told him; and Abraham built
the altar there, and arranged the wood,
and bound his son Isaac, and laid him
on the altar on top of the wood. And
Abraham stretched out his hand, and
took the knife to slay his son. But the
angel of the Lord called to him from
heaven and said, 'Abraham, Abraham!'
And he said, 'Here I am.' And he said,

'Do not stretch out your hand against the lad, and do nothing to him; for now I know that you fear God, since you have not withheld your son, your only son, from Me.' Then Abraham raised his eyes and looked, and behold, behind him a ram caught in the thicket by his horns; and Abraham went and took the ram, and offered him up for a burnt offering in the place of his son. And Abraham called the name of that place the Lord Will Provide, as it is said to this day, in the mount of the Lord it will be provided.

"Then the angel of the Lord called to Abraham a second time from heaven, and said, 'By Myself I have sworn, declares the Lord, because you have done this thing, and have not withheld your son, your only son, indeed I will greatly bless you, and I will greatly multiply your seed as the stars of the heavens, and as the sand which is on the seashore; and your seed shall possess the gate of their enemies. And in your seed all the nations of the earth shall be blessed, because you have obeyed my voice'"
(Genesis 22:1-18).

In this story, we see that Abraham did not even question God when He told him to sacrifice his son, whom Abraham loved and was told would have great blessings in his life. Abraham simply told Isaac that God would provide. In fact, this story is where God is first referred to as Jehovah Jireh, our Provider. I submit to you that He is our provider when we are obeying His voice! This is a revelation that can change your life perspective.

Many people want the blessings of God and the abundant life Jesus shared; but to achieve all that God has planned for you, you must be willing to listen to His voice and to live your life in a manner that obeys His direction. I believe God has given gifts and talents to every person and that He wants everyone to utilize them in building the kingdom for Him. Jesus said, *"You did not choose Me but I chose you, and appointed you that you would go and bear fruit, and that your fruit would remain" (John 15:16).* When we see that our purpose here on earth is to please Him and bear fruit in our lives, we can ask Him for direction on how we can play our part. A loving Father would not withhold from us what He wants us to do.

I will share how we can do this in practical ways by sharing real-life stories, but first let me share another Scripture that proves that it is through our obedience that the blessings come:

"Now it shall be, if you will diligently obey the Lord your God, being careful to do all His commandments which I command you today, the Lord your God will set you high above all the nations of the earth. And all these blessings shall come upon you and overtake you, if you will obey the Lord your God.

"Blessed shall you be in the city, and blessed shall you be in the country.

"Blessed shall be the offspring of your body and the produce of your ground and the offspring of your beasts, the increase of your herd and the young of your flock.

"Blessed shall be your basket and your kneading bowl.

"Blessed shall you be when you come in, and blessed shall you be when you go out.

"The Lord will cause your enemies to rise against you to be defeated before you; they shall come out against you one way and shall flee before you seven ways. The Lord will command the blessing upon you in your barns and in all that you put your hand to, and He will bless you in

the land which the Lord your God gives you. The Lord will establish you as a holy people to Himself, as He swore to you, if you will keep the commandments of the Lord your God, and walk in His ways. So all the peoples of the earth shall see that you are called by the name of the Lord; and they shall be afraid of you. And the Lord will make you abound in prosperity, in the offspring of your body and in the offspring of your beast and in the produce of your ground, in the land which the Lord swore to your fathers to give you. The Lord will open for you His good storehouse, the heavens, to give rain to your land in its season and to bless all the work of your hand; and you shall lend to many nations, but you shall not borrow. And the Lord shall make you the head and not the tail, and you only shall be above, and shall not be underneath, if you will listen to the commandments of the Lord your God, which I charge you today, to observe them carefully and do not turn aside from any of the words which I command you today, to the right or to the left, to go after other gods to serve them" (Deuteronomy 28:1-14).

Moses wrote this to the children of Israel to teach them how to live their lives as they entered the Promised Land. I believe the verses apply to us today as well. The promised blessings are in our coming and going, our homes and businesses, our families and everything that happens to us. Sounds like the abundant life to me! But the key is in verses one and two where it says that these blessings shall come upon us if we diligently obey God.

Similarly, just after this passage in Deuteronomy 28, Moses also talks about prosperity and choosing life and blessing instead of death and the curse:

> *"Then the Lord your God will prosper you abundantly in all the work of your hand, in the offspring of your body and in the offspring of your cattle and in the produce of your ground, for the Lord will again rejoice over you for good, just as He rejoiced over your fathers; if you obey the Lord your God to keep His commandments and His statutes which are written in this book of the law, if you turn to the Lord your God with all your heart and soul.*

> *"For this commandment which I command you today is not too difficult for you, nor is it out of reach. It is not in*

heaven, that you should say, 'Who will go up to heaven for us to get it for us and make us hear it, that we may observe it?' Nor is it beyond the sea, that you should say, 'Who will cross the sea for us to get it for us and make us hear it, that we may observe it?' But the word is very near you, in your mouth and in your heart, that you may observe it.

"See, I have set before you today life and prosperity, and death and adversity; in that I command you today to love the Lord your God, to walk in His ways and to keep His commandments and His statutes and His judgments, that you may live and multiply, and that the Lord your God may bless you in the land where you are entering to possess it. But if your heart turns away and you will not obey, but are drawn away and worship other gods and serve them, I declare to you today that you shall surely perish. You will not prolong your days in the land where you are crossing the Jordan to enter and possess it. I call heaven and earth to witness against you today, that I have set before you life and death, the blessing and the curse. So choose life in

> *order that you may live, you and your de-*
> *scendants, by loving the Lord your God,*
> *by obeying His voice, and by holding*
> *fast to Him; for this is your life and the*
> *length of your days, that you may live*
> *in the land which the Lord swore to your*
> *fathers, to Abraham, Isaac, and Jacob,*
> *to give them" (Deuteronomy 30:9-20).*

Moses is saying here that life and blessings are a choice that we are allowed to make, but there is a qualifier for achieving it: obey the Lord your God. Also, notice that he says in this passage that this *"is not too dif-ficult, nor is it out of reach" (Deuteronomy 30:11).* I spend a lot of time with college students and young adults, and one of the biggest questions they have is how to hear from God. The first thing I want them to understand is that it is not too difficult, nor is it out of reach.

Moses also says in this passage that if we turn to God with all our heart and soul, we will have abundant prosperity. This is another passage that puts the two words 'soul' and 'prosperity' together, and notice that it says this abundance happens if we obey the Lord (Deuteronomy 30:10).

Before I share additional Scriptures that further prove that obeying God leads to the abundant life, let me clarify what prosperity should mean to the Christian

45

who is hungry for God. Many people are seeking fortune and fame through material possessions, but that is not the angle I see here. God is very clear that material blessings can come upon us if we are obeying Him, but let's understand why He would give us material blessings:

> *"For when God made the promise to Abraham, since He could swear by no one greater, He swore by Himself, saying, 'I will surely bless you, and I will surely multiply you.' And so, having patiently waited, he obtained the promise. For men swear by one greater than themselves, and with them an oath given as confirmation is an end of every dispute. In the same way God, desiring even more to show to the heirs of the promise the unchangeableness of His purpose, interposed with an oath, so that by two unchangeable things in which it is impossible for God to lie, we may have strong encouragement, we who have fled for refuge in laying hold of the hope set before us. This hope we have as an anchor of the soul, a hope both sure and steadfast and one which enters within the veil"* (Hebrews 6:13-19).

We see here that God was very serious about this promise that He made to Abraham, so serious that the Bible says, "He swore by Himself." This emphasis illustrates how important this promise was to God. Two thousand years after the Hebrews passage was written, we can see that the offspring of Abraham is too many to count. The book of Hebrews also says that we can have this hope as 'an anchor of our soul'. What is the hope? That surely He will bless us and surely He will multiply us!

Paul says to the church in Galatia that if we are believers in Christ, we are heirs to this same promise that God gave to Abraham. *"And if you belong to Christ, then you are Abraham's offspring, heirs according to promise" (Galatians 3:29).*

These two passages from Galatians and Hebrews show that the promise of blessings and prosperity are available to believers today. Obviously, not every Christian is living in this abundance, so where is the breakdown? I believe it lies in two problem sources: first, not knowing how to hear (and consequently, to obey) God's voice; and second, not knowing the purpose of the prosperity as well as the purpose of the blessings. We will get into practical ways of how to hear His voice, but first let's figure out what the purpose of this promise to Abraham was.

When we first read about the story of Abraham, when he was still known as Abram, God called him and gave him a promise:

> *"Now the Lord said to Abram, 'Go forth from your country, and from your relatives, and from your father's house, to the land which I will show you; and I will make you a great nation, and I will bless you, and make your name great; and so you shall be a blessing; and I will bless those who bless you, and the one who curses you I will curse. And in you all the families of the earth shall be blessed'"* (Genesis 12:1-3).

God blessed Abraham abundantly for his obedience and then gave the same promise of blessing to his descendants, so they could also receive these blessings. But this promise was made to both Abraham and his descendants for one purpose, and that is that they could be a blessing to the families of the earth. In other words, God has promised blessings so that we can bless others. If it is true that this is God's desire, then it stands to reason that if we are using our gifts, talents, and resources to be a blessing to others, then God will speak to us about where and how we are to use these resources. If we decide- because we are given a free will to make decisions- to use our God-given resources for our own purposes, then I believe God will move His blessings on to someone else who will be more obedient.

God's purpose through us on this earth is not just to give us an easy life and then let us live forever in heaven. His purpose is to see as many people as possible enter into a relationship with Him so there are more people who can spend eternity with Him. He can only accomplish this purpose through us, His people. It takes resources to reach people, and God is eagerly willing to give these resources to those who are all about loving people and helping others come into that relationship with Him. As *2 Chronicles 16:9 says, "The eyes of the Lord move to and fro throughout the earth that He may strongly support those whose heart is completely His."*

For our heart to be completely God's, then we need to be willing to hear Him and obey Him with all our decisions. We must realize that God does know the future and He does know what is best for us, so trusting Him to guide us is safe because, as a Father, He really does want the best for us. It just needs to involve His passion, which is seeking out and saving the lost.

When people ask me why I believe in God, it is not because someone told me about Him or because I read about Him in a book. I believe in God because I have seen Him break addictions in my life and change me radically from where I was. I have seen so many miracles that cannot be explained in any other way except to believe that there is a God who cares and is engaged in orchestrating the affairs of His kids.

There are many areas of our lives where we can be blessed, including our business and career. Allow me to share my career story so you can see how God has spoken to me many times about my career. As I have obeyed and stepped out in faith, He has blessed every move I have made.

When I first got saved, I felt such a burden to be in full-time ministry. I had graduated with a degree, yet I still was not convinced of what I should do with my life. I had an opportunity to go on a mission trip to Manila, Philippines, just after graduating.

This trip would have a major impact on me and my direction in life. I went with the purpose of seeking God every day and believing that He would reveal to me what to do next. We worked hard every day and saw literally hundreds of people come to know the Lord. I was interested in moving there and doing this type of ministry permanently, but was praying and asking God every morning to reveal His will. One morning while I was praying, I felt God tell me He was going to use me in business. I did not know what this meant or what it would look like. Our trip leader was Rice Broocks, who wrote the book *God Is Not Dead*, which became a movie. I spoke with Rice about this; he prayed and confirmed that he felt it was what God wanted me to do. I do believe there is wisdom in a multitude of counselors!

As I continued to pray, God also told me that He wanted me to stay in my college town of Auburn, Alabama and support my church. This presented some obstacles because there were not many engineering jobs there. It was a college town that was built around the university. But I wanted to obey God so that I could have His support in my life.

Every morning for six weeks I would get up and pray for about an hour and ask God for wisdom on what to do that day. We had no Internet then, so I went to the library and got a book that listed all the companies in each town within an hour of Auburn. I would call each company and ask if they were looking to hire any engineers. I was rejected by many companies, but I did receive some interviews and got some experience answering the questions that employers would ask.

Then, two weeks before my wedding, I called a manufacturing company one hour away who hired engineers regularly. They scheduled an interview and offered me a job on the spot. Immediately I was making more money than most of my fellow engineering graduates. The Personnel Manager later told me that previously they had never hired anyone in that manner. I truly believe that God was honoring the fact that I was willing to listen to Him and obey whatever He told me to do.

I also want to point out that I did not stay at home and expect God to bring a job to me. I went out and tried everything I could think of, and that is when God provided an opportunity. I believe God was testing my faith to see if I would really obey what He wanted me to do.

For seven years I worked as an engineer. I knew in my heart it wasn't what I was called to do for the rest of my life. I would pray often for God to direct me, and one thing He kept reminding me was that He wanted me to *"dwell in the land and cultivate faithfulness" (Psalm 37:3)*. To me this meant that, while I was waiting, I should *"do my work as unto the Lord" (Colossians 3:23)*. In other words, I felt God was honored if I would work hard and do everything I could to bring Him the credit. Because everyone found out quickly that I was a Christian, I wanted to be the hardest working person there.

During those seven years I was promoted multiple times. They moved me to four different plants. In one twelve-month period, I received three promotions. I don't say this at all to brag because the glory all goes to God. I had the worst GPA of every single engineer in the company and should have never been hired based on my grades. Sometimes I think God chuckles when He uses someone like me because it just doesn't make sense to the world!

Toward the end of the seven years I felt God was stirring in my heart that something was about to change. I was living in Georgia, but felt that God wanted me to move back to my hometown of Birmingham, Alabama. I had told my wife that it was the one city I never wanted to live in because of my past. I did not ever want to be around the people I grew up with and remember all the trouble. But again, I think God has a sense of humor. (We need to be careful not to limit God by saying what we will or will not do!)

There were no opportunities in Birmingham in my field, but I really did not want to continue in the engineering profession anyways. During my high school and college years, I had worked in the cable television business climbing telephone poles and hooking up cable to individual houses. This had helped me pay my way through college. I began to feel this would be an outlet that could get me back to Birmingham. It was very humbling to think that, with an engineering degree, I would go back to climbing telephone poles.

Because I kept feeling the pull towards Birmingham, I knew it was time to make a decision. I was six weeks away from getting a substantial bonus that was equal to twenty percent of my salary. Common sense would have told me to stay and make the decision later. But

God was pulling my heart. One day at lunch I went to the library, opened my Bible, started reading, and asked God what I should do. I would read for a while and then pray. "God, what do you want me to do? It makes no sense to leave now, but I want to obey You and do Your will."

As I sat there, I would read for a while and pray. And I heard nothing. Then, as I was reading, I said, "God what do you want me to do?" And I felt Him say, "I want you to go." I prayed, "Lord, do you want me to quit my job and go to Birmingham?" And in my heart, I felt Him say, "Yes." I prayed, "Lord, do you want me to quit my job, walk away from this bonus, and move to Birmingham?" Again, I heard, "Yes." I went back to my first memorized verse, *Proverbs 3:5-6: "Trust in the Lord with all your heart, and lean not on your own understanding, in all your ways acknowledge Him and He will make your paths straight."* I simply trusted that this was what He wanted me to do. I closed my Bible and went back to work.

That night I told my wife what I believed God wanted us to do. She was excited and also felt it was what God wanted. One of her favorite verses says, *"wisdom from above is first pure, then peaceable, gentle, reasonable, full of mercy and good fruits, unwavering, without hypocrisy" (James 3:17)*. We both felt a peace about this, even though it made no sense in our minds yet.

I contacted the owner of the cable contracting company where I had worked years before and asked if I could come back to work for him. He laughed and said that he had no engineering jobs. I told him I would be willing to start at the bottom and climb telephone poles and hook cable to houses again. Because I had always been a hard worker, he said he would have a job for me if I moved.

This was one of the most humbling things I had done in my life. Climbing poles and crawling under houses was not why I spent years in college. But I knew God wanted me back in Birmingham. Though I didn't fully understand the reason yet, I wanted to continue to obey Him. Each day I worked hard while trying to figure out why God had called me to Birmingham. Within a few weeks of moving to Alabama, an opportunity presented itself to relocate again and run a project in Mississippi, which I accepted. This opportunity opened doors that would not have been available if I had not humbled myself and obeyed God.

Within a few months, I had started my own contracting company and had over one hundred contractors working in twelve different states. Seven years earlier God had told me that He would use me in business. It was starting to become clearer that God had gifted me with running businesses, and I needed to make sure that I was seeking His purpose in this rather than running after my own agenda.

I continued in the cable business for four years and saw more financial success than I had ever imagined. But God began stirring in me again that there was something else for me. One day on a flight home from Houston, Texas, where I had an office, I felt in my heart that God wanted me to walk away from the business. At the time I was doing better financially than I had ever done. Looking at the numbers alone, it made no sense for me to quit. But, being honest with myself, some of the things I was seeing in the business were not ethical. People were expecting kick-backs for awarding contracts, and I wanted no part of that. I knew in my heart that if God wanted me to change careers again, He would provide for me. I will continue with this story in a moment.

In this book I am trying to help you understand how God can take your life from average, or good, to great. I firmly believe that a life with God's strong support, as 2 Chronicles says, is only available as we are obeying God for the direction in our lives. When we put our trust in Him to direct our paths and look for ways to fulfill the purpose for which He created us, we can see Him move in ways that defy reason.

Many people remind me of the story of the spider monkey. The spider monkey lives in the forests in South America. The natives will catch the spider monkey because he will lead them to water. If they hold him long enough to make him thirsty, he will run directly to water when they let him go. But how do they catch him? They bury a clay jar in the ground that has a narrow neck on it. They then place a banana in the jar. When the spider monkey reaches in and grabs the banana, he cannot remove his hand from the jar, and will not let go of the banana and so he is caught. All he would have had to do is let go of the banana, but he holds onto it because he fails to see that releasing it is the only way to freedom.

I see people limit their opportunities because they are holding onto something that is meaningful to them, not realizing it may be keeping them from having God's best in their lives. Maybe it is a relationship, or a job, or living in a particular city, but one thing I have learned throughout my life is that it is much easier to hear God when I do not put limits on Him. In other words, God does not want me to say, "Lord, I'll move anywhere as long as it isn't Birmingham," or "I'll do anything You ask, as long as I can keep my job," or, "I'll follow You as long as I can keep dating this person." God wants us to take away all the barriers and just trust Him.

When I asked my wife to marry me, I asked her a very important question that would be tested throughout our marriage. I asked her how she would respond if God told us to sell everything we had and live in a tent as a missionary. She immediately told me that she would do it. I needed to hear this because I knew this was how I wanted to live my life. God has never asked me to live in a tent, but He has had me sell my house, downsize, and change careers multiple times. Each time it would have been easier to reason with God how we should have just kept doing what we were doing. But then I believe God would have found someone else to throw His support to and use in a way that would serve His purpose.

So after much prayer and consultation with men I trusted about the changing cable industry culture, I walked away from a business that was paying more money than I thought you could make in a year. Many of my friends thought I was crazy, but I knew it was what God wanted and that He would provide for me. I had two young children at the time, which did not make this decision any easier. I spent several months selling equipment I had purchased and seeking God on what was next.

One day as I was praying, I felt God telling me to start a home construction company. I loved building things, but knew very little about building houses, so this presented some challenges. But I obeyed God and jumped in. In the same year, a door was opened for me to buy a decorative concrete business, which would also turn out to be quite lucrative. Both of these companies began to grow. Four years later, I had a tough decision to make. I had expanded the concrete business to four states and, because of the success, the owner of the company offered me the position of distributor for a third of his business. This was a major opportunity, but I realized I would not be able to run both companies any longer. I had to choose one.

The construction company was growing, but was not making the money he was offering. If I had been looking just at the financial end of the decision, it would have been easy. But again, I had learned to trust God in my life and have seen Him move in miraculous ways. My wife and I both prayed and we both believed God wanted us to leave the concrete business and focus on the construction business. When I called the owner of the company to inform him of my decision, he could not believe it. He didn't understand how I could turn down such a good deal. But God's ways are not man's ways, and sometimes doing what God wants does not make sense in the natural.

I have now been running the construction company for over 21 years and survived the housing recession of 2007-2012 — a recession that wiped out most of the builders in my city. When I look back on why God would have me change careers so many times, I am convinced it is because He wanted to make sure it was never about me. He has given me talents and gifts to run a business, but He wanted to make sure I was not just chasing the money. Each time I walked away from a business was when I was making the most money in it. Although I went backwards financially each time, the next endeavor always became better than the prior one.

This is how I see the abundant life God desires for us. He sees around the corners of life and always wants what is best for His kids, but He wants us doing things for the right reasons- always staying focused on loving Him and loving people. When we put our trust in Him for the big decisions in life, we will see our lives grow in ways we never could have imagined.

When you look around and find someone who appears to have God's strong support in his or her life, you will see that his or her success is not common and is not found often. When you find this person, oftentimes you will also find someone who has trusted God with a big decision and been obedient to what He wanted him or her to do.

A great example is my Senior Pastor, Chris Hodges. The church he started, Church of the Highlands, presently has 17 different campuses around the state of Alabama with over 40,000 people attending services each week. It is easy to see that this church has been blessed by God. For example, in two recent weeks, the church has hosted two big events. One was a Motion conference where 16,000 students came together for three days to hear from some of the top speakers in the world and worship with some of the top worship bands, including Hillsong Young and Free, David

Crowder, and Passion Worship. This conference is held every summer to prepare the students to go back to school ready to take a bold stand for Jesus.

The second conference was for over 4,300 pastors from around the world, coming together for three days of workshops in addition to training on how to go back and grow their churches. This conference is also held each summer, and has been overwhelmingly success-ful in empowering churches worldwide. It is exciting to see these pastors leave with tools to help their churches grow to levels they had not yet experienced.

Church of the Highlands is also involved in nineteen of the state correctional facilities, where we have weekly services to help the inmates. Additionally, we hold an annual Serve Day in the summer where over 10,000 people go all around the city and serve the community in tangible ways, like cutting grass, painting schools, and helping literally thousands of people who need help. It is truly the best example I have ever witnessed of the church doing what it was called to do in a city to make a difference.

None of this would have happened if it wasn't for Pastor Chris hearing from God and taking a bold step to be obedient. He was doing a great job as a youth pastor in Baton Rouge, Louisiana. It would have been easy to stay there with his five children and keep do-ing what he was doing. He also had an opportunity to be the lead pastor in an established church in another state. But while he was attending a baseball tournament in Birmingham, he felt God spoke to him that he would pastor a church there. After praying and seeking advice, he knew this was what the Lord wanted him to do.

Pastor Chris could have been successful anywhere he went. He is very gifted at communicating- taking truths from the Bible and making them understandable. But I truly believe that the amazing success he has seen at Church of the Highlands, which is known around the world, is due to his obedience to God. He was willing to let go of a good life and obey God so that he could see God use his talents in the greatest way possible. Because of this obedience, thousands upon thousands of people have come into a real relationship with God.

As you are reading this, you may be wondering why you haven't been able to hear God speak in such a clear way. Let me explain a practical way for you to start hearing from God. I learned this technique from a book, *The Pursuit of God*, by A.W. Tozer. I read this book while I was in college, shortly after becoming a Christian. Tozer never graduated from high school or college, but was self-taught. He authored many books and pastored churches for most of his adult life.

He states in this classic book, "It is important that we get still to wait on God. And it is best that we get alone, preferably with our Bible outspread before us. Then if we will we may draw near to God and begin to hear Him speak to us in our hearts."

Also, "If you would follow on to know the Lord, come at once to the open Bible expecting it to speak to you. Do not come with the notion that it is a thing which you may push around at your convenience. It is more than a thing; it is a voice, a word, the very Word of the Living God."

Tozer is saying that to hear from God we must get still before Him with our Bible open and expect Him to speak to us. Remember that Jesus said, *"My sheep hear My voice" (John 10:27)*. Jesus also said that He would send the Holy Spirit to live inside of us, to teach us how to live, to bring to our remembrance all that Jesus said to us (John 14:26). It takes faith to believe these truths, but by exercising our faith and trusting what God has said in His Word, we can begin to hear His voice.

Hebrews 4:12 says, *"For the word of God is living and active and sharper than any two-edged sword."* When we simply open the Bible and read it, expecting God to speak to us, He will. Before we read, we can pray and ask God to reveal things that He wants us to know. It often amazes me how something I read that was written thousands of years ago applies directly to my life today.

You may start by praying to God, "Lord, as I read today, please show me something You want me to know, or to do." I believe God will hear this prayer and begin to show you truths He wants you to know. This is how we begin to hear His voice. And as we are obedient, He will take us deeper and deeper into what He wants us to know. The key point is to not overthink this or try to hear an audible voice. It is typically more like a still, small voice that gently whispers as you are reading and seeking Him.

Jesus told us to seek first the kingdom of God and "all these things" would be added to us (Matthew 6:33). The "things" He was referring to were the necessities of life, like food, clothing, and shelter. He said to not worry about them, but rather seek God first and He would provide. If God is concerned about our basic necessities being met, doesn't it stand to reason that He would also be concerned about whom we will marry and where we should live and work? Of course it does, so we should keep our focus on God first and then He will begin to speak to us about our lives.

Having children is a great way to understand how incredible God's love is for us. For example, I opened a sweet note that came in the mail from one of my daughters just thanking me for some things I had done. She finished the note with the phrase, "I am honored to be your daughter." There are just not many accolades I could ever achieve in life that could take the place of that! Don't you think that is how God feels about us? Instead of constantly asking Him for favors, we should just thank Him for what He has already done. We should seek His will and not our own will for our lives. As we practice this and focus on Him first, He will reveal the answers we need in the proper timing.

In the first two chapters of this book, I have shown the importance of staying in the Word and then learning to obey God. These two chapters tie together because you can learn to hear God by continuing to read and meditate on the Bible, expecting God to speak.

The next three habits we will discuss will explain how to keep the enemy from wreaking havoc in our lives. If we want to live the abundant life that Jesus came to give us, then we need to uncover these truths and act upon them. As James said, *"But prove yourselves doers of the Word, and not merely hearers who delude themselves" (James 1:22)*.

3

Habit Number Three
Fasting

"Then you will call, and the Lord will
answer; you will cry for help, and He
will say: Here am I." Isaiah 58:9

If we want to have success in every area of our life
and achieve the abundant life that Jesus described,
then we need to meditate on the Bible. Then we need
to be careful to do what is in it. This next habit we
will discuss was never talked about in Sunday School
when I was young. As a matter of fact, I had never
heard the word or understood the concept when I got
saved. But when I read it in my Bible, I began to see
that it was something God wanted me to do.

In this chapter I will discuss what fasting is, why we should fast, the many benefits of fasting, and then end with some very practical ways on how to fast. If this is a new concept to you, don't worry! It was new to me when I got saved. Allow me to share with you some truths in the Bible about how this is supposed to be an important part of our Christian life, and I believe you will see some benefits. Remember, we are all seeking to please God with our lives and live the abundant life Jesus came to give us, so we must learn to be obedient to what the Bible tells us. The ultimate goal as Christians is to give the world reasons to look at us and desire the life we live so they can taste the freedom and peace that comes with knowing God. There is a hurting world out there that needs to know what we know, and when you get right down to it, that is where God's heart always is: to seek and save that which is lost!

Fasting is not just for monks who are hidden in the hills, but is for anyone willing to be used to accomplish the greatest amount of good for God's purpose. Quite frankly, God paid too big a price on the cross for me to not want to obey everything He has laid out for me to do.

There are many instances in the Bible where people fasted when they needed help, or were going into battle, or because someone was just desperate to hear from God. We will discuss these. But keep in mind that Jesus fasted for forty days before He started His ministry. He went into the wilderness and went without food; when He came back He launched His ministry and found His initial twelve disciples whom He would use to change the world. The point is that we don't have to wait until there is a crisis in our lives, or a big need. We can begin the habit of fasting so we are prepared when the trials come.

Let's first understand what fasting is. It is a time of going without food when we can clear our minds and seek God. It is a time to get our focus off the world and onto God. It can be for a day, a week, or longer, but we should never look to fast for more than a few days without first counseling with a medical professional. God does not want us to be foolish: if you have a medical condition, you must be careful not to push physical limits.

I love how Pastor Jentezen Franklin explains fasting in his book, *Fasting*:

> "When you fast, you abstain from food for spiritual purposes. I've heard people say that they were planning to fast TV or computer games or surfing the Internet. It is good to put those things down for a time of consecration if they're interfering with your prayer life or with your study of God's Word or your ministering to the needs of

> others, but technically, that is not fasting. Fasting is doing without food for a period of time which generally causes you to leave the commotion of normal activity. Part of the sacrifice of fasting, seeking God, and studying his Word is that normal activity fades into the background."

At Church of the Highlands, we have a 21-day period of prayer and fasting every January. There are many churches around the world that do this. We do this in January because there are several references in the Bible about putting God first in our lives. During this time, we are all encouraged to seek the Lord for the next year by fasting and praying. We gather each morning at 6:00 a.m. to worship and pray together. Over the years, this has proven to be a time when God has spoken to me in key areas of my life where I needed direction. This clear direction comes from being intentional with getting my mind off the things of the world for a set period.

This is also a great time to form better habits. As Jentezen Franklin said in the above quote, fasting is not just giving up TV or social media — it is giving up food for a set period of time and seeking God. However, I do believe there are significant benefits in our spiritual lives when we discipline ourselves to withhold something that is important to us, and I believe God honors that.

As I mentioned earlier in the book, studies show that it takes 21 days to form a habit. Before I start the 21 days of prayer and fasting each year, I consider the activities in my life where I am spending my time. For the 21 days, I will stop doing an activity that is important to me. I do this to let God know that He is more important to me than anything else in my life. After 21 days, it is often interesting when I see how easy it is to live without the particular activity! It has also led to changes in how I spend my time through-out the year.

But again, this is more for discipline purposes and not at the root of fasting. I can attribute many successes in my life- such as getting direction, hearing from God about specific things, and breaking bondages- to fasting food on a regular basis for over the past thirty years. We will discuss each of these in this chapter, but I want to remind you that the purpose of this book is to help anyone willing to set some discipline habits in their lives to be able to achieve the abundant life that Jesus said He came to give us.

If fasting is not some spiritual diet we do to lose weight, then why should we fast? First, it is an act of obedience to God. It clears our mind and gets our focus off the world. Many times, we think about food so much that it becomes more important than God. Fasting puts it back in perspective and lets your physical body know that its lusts and desires are not in control. It also helps keep our focus on the things that really matter. Paul instructs, *"Present your bodies a living and holy sacrifice; acceptable to God, which is your spiritual service of worship" (Romans 12:1).*

In his book, Jentezen Franklin says, "The discipline of fasting will humble you, remind you of your dependency on God, and bring you back to your first love. It causes the roots of your relationship with Jesus to go deeper."

There are many reasons to fast, as well as many benefits, but the simplest and easiest to understand is that Jesus told us to do so. In the last chapter, we saw that true success in life comes when we are obedient to God. If we believe this, then we should look at what the Bible tells us to do and then do it, especially if Jesus tells us to.

When Jesus started His three-year ministry with the disciples, He gathered with them and gave them a few principles, often referred to as the Sermon on the Mount. This sermon is recorded in Matthew 5-7. It is full of instruction on how to live. When He finished speaking, the multitudes were amazed at His teaching, for He was teaching as one having authority (Matthew 7:28-29).

During this sermon Jesus told the people that when they gave, they were not to sound a trumpet to be heard by men, but should give in secret and that their reward would be with God. He then said that when they prayed, they should not do it to be seen by men, but should pray in secret and the Father would see it and repay them. He said that when they fasted, they were not to put on a gloomy face, but again, do it in secret and the Father would repay them. Each time He instructed them not to do these things to be seen by men, but to do them in secret to be seen by God, and that God would repay them.

The big point I want you to see in this important passage is that Jesus did not instruct them 'if' they give, or 'if' they pray, or 'if' they fast. He instructed them, 'when' they give, and 'when' they pray, and 'when' they fast. He was saying to all the people listening that these were things they were to do- not to get any favors from men who see it, but to have God see it in private so that their rewards will come from Him.

Also notice that He shared this message not only to His twelve disciples, but also to the multitudes at the Sermon on the Mount. He was laying a foundation for how we are to live as followers of Jesus. This still applies today to believers.

In the previous chapter we discussed learning to hear from God, so that we can obey Him. We also saw in the Bible that, as we obey Him, we can achieve the abundant life Jesus spoke about. Think of hearing and obeying God being like a muscle: the more you practice and use it, the easier it becomes to hear Him speak. A simple way to start this process is to pray before you open His Word and ask that He will reveal something to you that you should do. Then, as you are reading, and you come across an instruction, ask God if it applies to you.

In other words, when we see Jesus tell the multitudes to fast in a particular way in secret, we should simply ask God if this is something we should do. You can believe with certainty that if you feel it is something to try, then it is not your flesh and it is not the devil telling you to do it. (In fact, we will discuss many reasons that the devil does not want you to fast!) Having this simple faith in hearing God and then acting upon it is how we begin to hear Him more easily in the future.

Have you ever had this situation happen to you? Someone asks for your advice, and you feel it is very clear what they should do, so you tell them your opinion. Then they go away and don't do it. But they come back later and again ask what they should do without heeding your previous advice! It makes you not want to help this person because they didn't listen to your advice in the first place.

Doesn't it make sense that perhaps God is that way? Maybe God has clearly told us to do certain things and we haven't done them, but we are constantly asking what to do next. Or maybe we are constantly praying for God to answer a prayer and there is something He has already told us to do, but instead we are focused on something else.

Sometimes He just wants us to be obedient to what He said to do in the first place. This begins with studying the Bible so that we can be careful to do what is written in it. When Jesus says we are to fast, we should just take it in faith that there is a reason He wants us to fast. We should ask Him how and when we should fast; He will give us a peace about the right direction, and then we should just obey Him and do what we feel He is saying. Remember, Jesus sent the Holy Spirit to live inside of us to bring to remembrance things that Jesus spoke to us. When we are studying the Bible and come across a verse that instructs us about *something* and we feel God wants us to do *that something*, we should understand that this is how the Holy Spirit begins to speak to us. He speaks softly, nudging us in a certain direction. As we exercise this process like a muscle, it becomes stronger and stronger until it becomes easy to hear from God.

When the disciples of John the Baptist came to Jesus to ask Him why His disciples did not fast, He answered that the time would come when they would fast. *"The attendants of the bridegroom cannot mourn as long as the bridegroom is with them, can they? But the days will come when the bridegroom is taken away from them, and then they will fast"* (Matthew 9:15).

We could end this chapter here and just say to start fasting because Jesus said to and that would be it settled. But I want to take some time to show you many benefits that come from fasting and how it has had eternal impacts on my life as well as those around me.

Benefits of Fasting

❖ It breaks bondage

During my first year as a Christian, I read my Bible completely through twice. I could not get enough of it because I felt it was giving me the instructions on how to live a life free of addictions, and showing me that by creating certain habits my life could be better than if I just sat back and let life happen to me. One of these habits I formed during this time was fasting. Fasting intrigued me because I had never heard about it, yet the Bible talked about how people would fast when they needed a breakthrough in their life or an answer to an important situation.

When I read that Jesus told us to fast, I started to cross reference all the verses in the Bible related to fasting. As with my "soul" and "prosperity" word search, I again used the Concordance to understand better about fasting. (With the Internet today, this is much easier!)

I saw in Isaiah and in Matthew two passages that tell us fasting can break bondages in our lives. This was something I definitely needed in my life because of the addictions I was bound in prior to getting saved. I have never fallen back since that October night in 1983, but that doesn't mean there weren't some struggles. If you have ever known someone who struggled with addiction, you probably know how hard it is to beat it. I have had family members who struggled their entire adult lives and went through multiple drug rehabs who never beat the addictions. The only times I have seen it work is when God has intervened in a big way. That is what happened to me.

Matthew 17 tells a story about how a man came to Jesus, desperate for his son to be healed. His son had a demon that would torment the boy, even throwing him into a fire. The disciples had prayed for him, but nothing happened. When the man brought his son to Jesus, Jesus rebuked the demon and it came out of the boy at once. When the disciples asked Jesus why they could not cast it out, Jesus answered, *"Because of the littleness of your faith; for truly I say to you, if you have faith as a mustard seed, you shall say to this mountain, 'Move from here to there,' and it shall move; and nothing shall be impossible to you. <u>But this kind does not go</u>*

out except by prayer and fasting" (Matthew 17:20-21, emphasis mine).

In America today, we don't often see demon possession, but it is real. It is not something we should simply dismiss as only existent in the Bible times. When Paul told us to take up the armor of God so that we could resist the devil, he told us that "our struggle is not against flesh and blood, but against the rulers, against the powers, against the world forces of this darkness, against spiritual forces of wickedness in the heavenly places" (Ephesians 6:12).

Fasting is also a way to fight these evil forces in our lives, and in the world today.

One of the best passages in the Bible regarding fasting is Isaiah 58. This chapter contains many promises about the results of fasting properly, but the one that first stuck out to me was how fasting could break bondages in our lives. Just as Jesus mentioned in the Sermon on the Mount, people in Isaiah's time were fasting to be seen by men, as if that was going to get them favor from men. The favor we should be seeking is from God, not other men. God told Isaiah to tell the people that they were not hearing from God during their fast because they were doing it with the wrong intentions, or motives. He said, "Is this not the fast which I choose, to loosen the bonds of wickedness, *to undo the bands of the yoke, and to let the oppressed go free, and break every yoke?" (Isaiah 58:6).*

This is exactly what I needed to hear to start fasting on a regular basis. I started fasting one day per week, and I give the credit to this habit for God breaking not only the addictions off my life, but the desire to ever participate in that life again. I saw the disaster addiction brought on me, and I wanted to be free. I found a habit that the Bible said would break every yoke in my life, so I committed to it. Was this me being legalistic, or trying to be super spiritual? No! I was desperate for a new life, and knew I had to take drastic measures to ever accomplish what God had in store for me.

If there is any struggle in your life and you want to change, I would suggest that you consider fasting and praying about it. Simply ask God if this is something you should do. If you feel that it is, then just be obedient and watch how God will use it. I believe that God will break any bondage that we have through this simple practice. It may seem hard at first, but once you have done it for a while, it will seem easier. The areas needing changed in your life may not be as drastic as mine were with addictions, but God wants us to live free from anything that keeps us from His best for us.

Drug addiction is easy to identify as wrong, but what about other, more subtle, areas in our lives where we are placing too much importance? Anything that is more important to us can become a god and take the place of importance that should only belong to God. Something as simple as spending too much time on social media can be an area that God wants to change for us. If we sense that God is nudging us to consider changing a habit so we can have a bigger impact for Him, then maybe fasting along with prayer is the answer. Jesus wants our lives to be abundant, and the only way for that to happen is for us to be sensitive to obeying God in every area of our lives. This is accomplished by fasting.

Another area that many don't like to mention is pornography. It is so easy now with the Internet to see things we shouldn't see. We may think that nobody is watching, but God sees everything we do in secret. Because I deal with young men a lot, I know this is a serious issue for them. I have seen people who were addicted to pornography, but have had God intervene and give them freedom. The best advice I could ever give to someone struggling with this is to fast and pray until the desire is no longer there. Trust me, it can definitely work!

It didn't take long for me to realize that this habit of fasting was working for me. But after getting the victory over my drug addiction, there was one burning desire that was at the top of my prayer requests. I had a brother, David, who was two years younger than me, and we were closer than any two brothers I have ever known. We grew up playing sports every day and then worked together in high school. It was hard on both of us when I went off to college. His life started spiraling down; he quit all sports and got more involved in drugs. He tried to come to college, but failed every course he took and quit within a few months of starting.

I felt a heavy burden because I had introduced David to drugs when he was a young teenager. I had seen the victory in my life and knew what it was like to go to sleep at night without the empty feeling left by drugs and alcohol; I desperately wanted David to experience that victory also. We also had an older brother, Derek, who didn't want David to leave the party scene and go "find religion," which is how he described my experience. For years Derek and I had this big spiritual tug-of-war over my younger brother. Because I had seen God move in my life in such a dramatic way, I knew I had to win this battle for David. It would have eternal ramifications, so I was going to do whatever I could.

As I saw how God had worked in my life, I began to believe that if I fasted and prayed for David, I could see God work in David's life as well. I began to set aside every Monday to fast, and to get in a quiet place, and pray that the strongholds of addiction would be broken over David's life. This went on for years. I did not fast every single Monday, but several times per month on average was common. I did it for one primary reason: to see David set free. Nobody ever knew this was happening except my wife (because I did not join her for dinner). I wanted no credit from anyone for doing this- I wanted my brother free!

Over the next 20 years I saw David continue to battle his addictions. He went through a tough divorce and had a hard time holding down jobs. I moved back to Birmingham against my desire because I felt God wanted me to be closer to my brother. It became a cycle: I would hire him in one of my companies where he would do great for a year or two, then get back on drugs and I would have to fire him. As you can probably imagine, this cycle caused our family gatherings to be negative because David was the baby in the family. For some reason, our parents thought I should have just been overlooking his problem. He went in and out of multiple rehabilitation centers, which usually had a short-term positive impact, but nothing permanent. In my opinion- after dealing with this closely for many years with many people close to me- I can say confidently that the only way for people to truly be set free is for God to intervene.

Many times, it would have been easy to just give up. I would receive phone calls at night from my mother that David had been involved in an accident and was in the hospital, or in jail, and she would ask if I would go get him. I often wondered when I might get that final call that he had killed himself. It tore me up inside to see this happening. But I couldn't give up fighting for his soul.

I felt in my heart that I was the only person who could reach David, and it was worth giving my life. I continued to pray and fast. Finally, after receiving another DUI, David decided to check into a Christian rehabilitation center called Rapha Ministries in Gadsden, Alabama. This is where David had a real encounter with the Lord and his life changed for eternity. The day I was to drive him there he drove my parent's car into a ditch and totaled it. I was so mad I could barely speak with him as we drove an hour to the facility.

After being there for six weeks, he was given a pass to have one visitor. My mom and dad desperately wanted to go see him, but he told them that he wanted me to come. I was hesitant because I had no contact with him to know where he was spiritually. But I agreed to come, and was I ever in for a pleasant surprise!

The reason David had wanted me to come was because he had genuinely gotten saved and God had broken the addiction off his life for good. David had finally made the decision that it was not possible in his own power, but that he must trust in the power of God to live this life of freedom I had been explaining to him for years. We spent the afternoon talking about his future, and I saw how my prayers had finally been answered. David sent me a letter the next week thanking me for coming. He told me how he had a new direction and excitement for life and for what God had in store for him. He wrote that he felt God was going to use him to minister to young men with drug problems and help them get over their addictions by trusting in God. I had never seen him so focused on where he was going.

One week after writing that letter, David passed away from a massive heart attack. When my mom and dad arrived at the hospital at 2:00am, the nurse asked them who Glenn was. They told her I was David's brother, and she said that he was asking for me as he passed away. I know with one hundred percent certainty that David is in heaven now, and I am so thankful that God spared his life in all the accidents, so he could finally get his salvation secured.

Shortly after David's passing, I was reading my Bible and saw the verse where Jesus said that if we are faithful with little, we would be faithful with much (Luke 16:10). He also said that if we were not faithful with money, God would not entrust us with true riches. As I read this, I felt the Holy Spirit say to me that, because I was faithful with fasting and praying for David, and faithful with my money (which we will talk about in the next chapter), God had given me the true riches: David's salvation. I can honestly say that there is no level of success that can take the place of having David's eternity secured.

This is exactly how I have learned to hear God. As I am sensitive to obey His Word and do what it says, He is faithful and gives me the desires of my heart. I have never desired anything more than my brother's salvation, and I believe God heard my prayers for years and granted that to me because of my obedience and faithfulness.

Many people battle addictions, and most reading this are likely affected by a family member or a friend who has an addiction. I have a soft spot in my heart for this because I know it is usually good people with a great future who just made some bad decisions. Some look down on the homeless man on the street, but I know it could just as easily have been me. Don't give up on that lost friend or family member! You may be the only link they have to know God.

To finish the story of my brother: when the day of the funeral came, the rehabilitation center shut down and sent all the men on a bus to be there. These guys had been so touched by David's story that they wanted to let our family know the impact he had on them. They wrote about 30 letters and gave them to us on how David was a father figure to them and how they were going to beat their addictions. It showed me how God is so faithful and will use anybody willing to be used.

My two daughters also prayed earnestly for David for years. They loved their uncle Dave. My mother asked me to speak at the funeral and, as hard as that was, I knew it was the right thing to do. I spoke about how I was in a war for years over David's soul and how the enemy had won many battles. But God allowed me to see victory in the war for David. As we walked out of the funeral home, my sweet daughter Melissa came up to me and told me that everything was okay because we had won the most important battle. My girls are both prayer warriors and know not to give up on people that God has put on their hearts to pray for. They have both seen many people come to know the Lord because of their diligence.

Again, I want to encourage you not to give up believing for that lost loved one. Fast for them. Get in a quiet place by yourself and pray for God to break the chains that bind them. Remind God of what He said in Isaiah. I don't believe this offends God, but rather, I believe He loves to see our faith when we say we believe that what He said many years ago can still apply to today. Let God know that you believe His Word and believe what the Scriptures say. Tell Him that you want the bondage removed from your life or from someone else's. I believe God is pleased with this kind of prayer.

❖ Protection for your family

When we become parents, we see a different level of love that is hard to understand until you bring someone into the world. I believe God gives us this love so that we can get a glimpse of the love He has for us. The Bible says that *"If you then, being evil, know how to give good gifts to your children, how much more shall your Father in heaven give what is good to those who ask Him?"* (*Matthew 7:11*). This tells me that the love He has for us is immense. I love my kids so much that I would die for them, and they know it! God already sent His Son to die for me so that I can know Him. Because I want to protect my children, I believe God wants me to be protected as well.

The history of the city of Jerusalem shows that the temple that Solomon had built around 960 BC stood until it was destroyed by Nebuchadnezzar in 586 BC. Nebuchadnezzar enslaved the Jewish people and sent them to Babylon. Several decades later- around 538 BC- Cyrus, King of Persia, issued a decree for the temple and the walls around the city to be rebuilt. Both Ezra and Nehemiah returned to help with this project.

There are two stories I want to share with you from this big event in Jewish history. The first is when Ezra was gathering the exiles together to leave Babylon and return to Jerusalem after the temple was finished.

Before they left, he proclaimed a fast so they would have safe travels. The Bible records it as follows:

> *"Then I proclaimed a fast there at the river of Ahava, that we might humble ourselves before our God to seek from Him a safe journey for us, our little ones, and all our possessions. For I was ashamed to request from the king troops and horsemen to protect us from the enemy on the way, because we had said to the king, 'The hand of our God is favorably disposed to all those who seek Him, but His power and His anger are against all those who forsake Him.' So we fasted and sought our God concerning this matter, and He listened to our entreaty" (Ezra 8:21-23).*

Notice that Ezra didn't just fast, but he prayed while fasting for safety for his family and his people. And God answered him! I believe from this story that fasting and praying for protection and safety for our family will get a response from God.

The second story is when Nehemiah gathered the Jews to rebuild the walls of the city that had lain desolate for years. When the work was underway, there was an uprising from the outside led by a man named Sanballat who didn't want to see them succeed in rebuilding the wall. Nehemiah could tell that the people were afraid, but he knew he was doing what God wanted him to do. Nehemiah said, *"When I saw their fear, I rose and spoke to the nobles, the officials, and the rest of the people: 'Do not be afraid of them; remember the Lord who is great and awesome, and fight for your brothers, your sons, your daughters, your wives, and your houses'"* (Nehemiah 4:14).

As the head of my household, I have always felt a responsibility for the well-being of my wife and my daughters. I believe it is my responsibility to stand on that wall in a spiritual sense and fight for them and to place a protection around them. There is an enemy out there who is always wanting to thwart God's plans and destroy the good works He is doing in our lives, as well as in the lives of those around us. But we cannot give in because our fight is not against flesh and blood, but against the forces of evil that would come against us. As Christian leaders, we must stand in the spiritual gap for those we love!

We can actually provide safety for our family through prayer and fasting. We don't have to simply respond to the things the world throws at us; we can prepare ourselves through fasting as Jesus did in the wilderness before the trials ever come, which they will. And as we do this, we can stand in faith that God will have our back. *"For the Lord will go before you, and the God of Israel will be your rear guard"* (Isaiah 52:12).

❖ Health and healing

Oftentimes in our lives, we will be in a situation where we are believing God for a healing either for ourselves, someone in our close family, or a personal friend. During these times we can pray and claim the promises in the Bible concerning healing. We can also claim the many times Jesus told us to ask God for things we need, and we will receive if we believe. The Bible is clear that if we ask anything according to God's will, He hears us and grants our requests. *"And this is the confidence which we have before Him, that, if we ask anything according to His will, He hears us. And if we know that He hears us in whatever we ask, we know that we have the requests which we have asked from Him"* (1 John 5:14-15).

Nevertheless, there are times when we just aren't receiving what we are asking. We know what the Bible says, and we believe it. But as Jesus said when he cast out the demon, sometimes it takes prayer and fasting. When we are desperate for something from God, we should be willing to try anything we see in the Scriptures.

In the passage of Isaiah 58 where it discusses the fast that God would choose, it says that after we fast we can receive healing. *"Then your light will break forth like the dawn, and your healing will quickly appear"* (Isaiah 58:8 NIV).

If you or a loved one are in desperate need of healing in some area, try fasting and seeing if God will answer your prayer. Sometimes our simple faith is what moves Him to act in our lives. Remind God when you are claiming what it says in this verse and let Him know that you are believing this for yourself. I believe this type of faith pleases Him.

❖ Hear from God

Another benefit of fasting that I see in the Bible is that we can hear from God. When we have an important decision to make, it is good to free ourselves from the worries of the world by getting quiet before God and fasting. I am amazed at how clear my mind becomes when I go just one day without food. I have often received guidance from God during these times. Again, in Isaiah's great chapter on fasting, Isaiah says:

> *"Then you will call, and the Lord will answer; you will cry, and He will say, 'Here I am.' If you remove the yoke from your midst… the Lord will continually guide you, and satisfy your desire in scorched places, and give strength to your bones; and you will be like a watered garden, and like a spring of water whose waters do not fail" (Isaiah 58:9, 11).*

When my son-in-law, Taylor Brown, was about to graduate from college and start his career in the Air Force, he was having feelings for my daughter, Melanie. He was 22 years old at the time and she was 19. They had gotten to know each other through a bunch of friends who hung out and went to church together. Although Melanie had feelings for Taylor, she was not looking for a dating relationship and told him so. This went on for a few months until they realized the feelings had not gone away, and talked about it again. They had not even been on a date together, but Taylor was thinking this could be a permanent relationship. Over his Christmas break, he went to a remote cabin and spent time alone with God. He fasted for several days, so he could receive direction in what he thought was one of the most important decisions of his life. Melanie also fasted during this time and prayed for direction.

After a few days of this, they both felt that their feelings for each other were more than just an attraction and that God was involved. They realized there was a peace surrounding the idea of a relationship. They talked about it and Melanie told Taylor she wanted him to first come and talk to me before they started dating. I was so honored when Taylor came to my home and we discussed what dating meant to him. He told me then that he felt this was going to be permanent. It is safe to say that this is not common for college students to come ask the father if they can date his daughter! The fact that he was seeking God's will and wanting to please Him first spoke volumes to me.

The same thing happened with my other son-in-law, Travis Jackson, a short time later. He came to Birmingham and asked permission to date my daughter, Melissa. We had the same talk about what dating meant and I realized that he wasn't needing a girl to date, but believed that Melissa was the person he was supposed to marry. I could tell by his convictions and could hear in his voice that he really believed God was in the middle of this.

This may sound totally strange to you to have young men ask permission to date my daughters in this current culture, but it really should be the norm and not the exception. I have always felt a huge responsibility to protect my family spiritually, physically, and emotionally. For me to pass that authority on to a young man, I needed to know that they took it as seriously as I do. I needed to know that they are willing to fast and pray, not just for the protection of my girls, but to be able to hear God for direction and for His will in their lives.

Remember in Chapter 2 when I said that true success comes when we are obedient to His voice? We need to be able to read the Bible, and then do what it tells us to do. This is how we begin to receive God's blessings in our lives: we obey what He is telling us to do. One of the areas where we can practice obedience is fasting. When we take the Bible at face value and simply do what it says, God will allow us to grow and mature as Christians, so we can have a bigger impact on those around us. We can grow from children needing milk to mature adults who can eat the meat of the Word (Hebrews 5:12).

I love how Pastor Jentezen Franklin puts it in *Fasting*: "I am convinced that we will never walk in the perfect will of God until we seek Him through fasting. When you present your body in this manner, you open yourself up to hear from God. You will prove or discover His good and perfect will for your life. Fasting prepares the way for God to give you fresh revelation, fresh vision, and clear purpose."

Elijah is another biblical example of a man who fasted in his desperation to hear from God. Elijah was running for his life from Jezebel, who had threatened to kill him. A quick background: when Ahab became king over Israel, his wife, Jezebel, ordered the execution of the Lord's prophets. Elijah challenged King Ahab and told him to bring the prophets of Baal out so that they could see who the true God is.

Elijah ordered altars to be set up. Then he told the 450 prophets of Baal to call upon their gods so that their gods could come down and consume the ox that was to be sacrificed. When nobody answered these false prophets, Elijah had the people pour water on his offering until the water was overflowing, and then called out to God. God sent a fire that consumed the entire altar, including the wood, the ox offering, even the stones and the dust!

When the people saw this, they seized the prophets of Baal and killed them. When Jezebel heard the news, she sent a message to Elijah that she would have him killed within one day. So, Elijah ran into the wilderness to seek the Lord. He knew his life was in danger, so he began to fast. The Bible says, *"So he arose and ate and drank, and went in the strength of that food 40 days and 40 nights to Horeb, the mountain of God. Then he came there to a cave, and lodged there; and behold, the word of the Lord came to him, and He said to him, 'What are you doing here, Elijah?'" (1 Kings 19:8-9)*.

Hopefully we never find ourselves in a position where our life is threatened for being a Christian. But we can be certain that trials will come in our lives, because they are promised. This is what strengthens our faith. I believe God allows trials sometimes, so we can learn to rely on Him and learn to seek Him earnestly. One of the best ways I have found to do this when I need an answer is through fasting. If you need to hear from God for a big decision in your life, try humbling yourself with fasting.

There is also the story of Daniel hearing from God after he had fasted for twenty-one days. Daniel had received a vision concerning the last days and was trying to understand what it meant. He had been fasting without any answers when another vision came to him. He saw a man standing in white linen and could hear his voice. The man said to Daniel:

> *"Do not be afraid, Daniel, for from the first day that you set your heart on understanding this and on humbling yourself before your God, your words were heard, and I have come in response to your words. But the prince of the kingdom of Persia was withstanding me for twenty-one days; then behold, Michael, one of the chief princes, came to help me, for I had been left there with the kings of Persia. Now I have come to give you an understanding of what will happen to your people in the latter days, for the vision pertains to the days yet future"*
> *(Daniel 10:12-14)*.

There are many great lessons in this passage. First, Daniel was desperate to hear from God to understand the vision he had received. So, he fasted for twenty-one days. Then he got his answer. This vision is one of the key prophesies that talk about kingdoms that will rise and fall, and then goes into detail about what will happen in the end times. Many of these prophesies from the vision have already come to pass. But some are still in the future.

Second, we also get a glimpse into the battles that go on in the unseen world. Remember how Paul explained that our battles were fought in the spiritual and not the physical realm. *"For our struggle is not against flesh and blood, but against the rulers, against the powers, against the world forces of this darkness, against the spiritual forces of wickedness in the heavenly places" (Ephesians 6:12)*. This Scripture points back to Daniel's experience.

The evil forces were obviously not wanting Daniel to get clarity on this vision because it illuminated what would happen in the future. The angel told Daniel, *"Do you understand why I came to you? But I shall now return to fight against the prince of Persia; so I am going forth, and behold, the prince of Greece is about to come. However, I will tell you what is inscribed in the writing of truth. Yet there is no one who stands firmly with me against these forces except Michael your prince" (Daniel 10:20-21)*. By studying this passage, we can understand how to pray when we are seeking God for something important in our life. The battle is against the forces of evil that are constantly trying to come against the things of God. We must know who we are as children of God and use our authority that God gave us. (We will discuss this more in the chapter on confessing the Word.)

The last great lesson I can see in this passage is that the answers don't always come fast. Many times, we are wondering why God hasn't answered our prayer yet, but this passage lets us know that God heard our prayer from the beginning and will answer in the proper time. Like Daniel, we need to just keep pressing in until the answer comes, which it will.

❖ He will restore what was taken

A final benefit of fasting I see in the Bible is God's promise that He will restore what was taken from us. Things don't always go as we want them to in this life, and it is comforting to know that we can call out to God for help when we feel life has thrown us a curveball.

Being in the construction business, the recession of 2008-2012 was devastating for our industry. Many great people were put out of business, and most of it was not their own fault. Banks were lending money to people to buy homes who could not afford them. This was a setup for disaster, and when it came it was brutal. (I will talk more in the next chapter about how God helped me through it.) Because I read the Bible regularly, I can see where God has made promises where He would restore what was taken from us. Joel 2 says, *"Return to Me with all your heart, and with fasting, weeping, and mourning. Then I will make up to you for the years that the swarming locust has eaten, the creeping locust, the stripping locust, and the gnawing locust"* (Joel 2:12, 25).

I believe we can stand on verses like this and claim them when we pray. If we will humble ourselves with fasting as well, it will increase our chances of victory. I am not naïve enough to think that all our prayers will be answered the way we want them to be. What I have learned, though, is that I want every tool in the toolbox working in my favor. If Jesus says our prayers are more effective when we support them with fasting, then I am all in!

I claimed this verse many times since those lean years, and now my business is more than double the size it was before the recession. And it is growing. I don't take the credit, because I know who I am, with all my faults. I just know I serve a big God who has given us all a blueprint for succeeding in this life. All we must do is understand it and be obedient.

❖ It can keep our appetites in check

A final benefit I see that comes from fasting is that it can help curb our appetites and desires. I am definitely not saying that we should fast as a form of dieting, but the apostle Paul exhorted us to *"buffet our body and make it our slave" (1 Corinthians 9:27)*. This means that we should not allow our appetites to always have their way. Believe me, if I ate everything I wanted to at all times, I would be very overweight. It is important for us to not allow our flesh to have all its desires.

Living in the South, it seems that most people are overweight. Much of this is probably due to the type of foods we eat, like fried foods. You can fry anything in the South and people will eat it- from pickles to Oreos! But that is not an excuse for letting ourselves get overweight. Paul told us in Timothy to *"discipline ourselves for the purpose of godliness" (1 Timothy 4:7)*. As Christians, we should be the most disciplined people we know. People should be drawn to us for the way we live our lives.

One of the most disciplined people I have ever known was a Mormon whom I worked with early in my career. This impacted me because I wanted to show people that Christians were also disciplined. We see in the Old Testament book of Daniel how Daniel was given favor by the king for interpreting dreams for him. But it also says that Daniel separated himself from others. *"Now Daniel so distinguished himself among the ad-ministrators and the satraps by his exceptional qualities*

that the king planned to set him over the whole kingdom"
(Daniel 6:3 NIV).

One of the exceptional qualities I believe they saw in Daniel was his discipline with eating. He would not allow the desire for all the king's food to lure him away from his convictions. It would have been much easier for him to just blend in with the crowd and eat at the king's table. However, because he didn't, he was given favor from the king and we are still reading about him over two thousand years later. It is doubtful that we would ever know anything about him if he hadn't been so disciplined.

How do we fast?

Now that we have seen the importance of fasting and the many benefits that come from fasting, I would like to end the chapter talking about some practical ways to fast. Most people I know who fast just set a period of time to go without food, just drinking water. This is what I do. Others will do what is called the "Daniel fast," which refers to the time Daniel went twenty-one days without eating the king's food and just ate vegetables and drank water. We don't know his exact diet, but the Bible does say that he didn't eat meat or drink wine from the king's table. Many believe that the Daniel fast includes fruits, vegetables, whole grains, nuts and seeds, and water to drink. It does not include meats, dairy products, sweets, leavened bread, processed foods, or any other beverages. This is a common fast that people do, especially if going for multiple days.

As for the duration of a fast, there are multiple variations shown in the Bible: from sunup to sundown, to one full day, three days, ten days, and even forty days. If you fast all food for more than a couple of days, you should certainly ask your doctor first, to make sure there are no medical reasons for you not to fast. God does not want us to be foolish.

The most important thing is that we are coming before God with a humble attitude and seeking Him for direction or whatever it is that we need. God is not so concerned with exactly how we fast, but He is concerned with us obeying His Word. He also is looking at our heart and the motive behind everything we do. Are we fasting to be seen by men, or to get some spiritual credit from God? We will probably be disappointed if it's for either of these reasons! We should fast instead for the reasons discussed in this chapter, and we should expect to get breakthroughs when we do.

The Bible says that God does not show favoritism (Romans 2:9). This tells us that if God did something for someone else- whether in the Bible, or just someone we know- then God is able and willing to do the same for us. He wants us to have faith that He can, and will, do what we ask Him. Consider *Hebrews 4:16 (NIV): "Let us then approach God's throne of grace with confidence, so that we may receive mercy and find grace to help us in our time of need."*

From this verse we can see that God wants us to come to Him with confidence that He will answer us. He loves us and wants us to have complete faith in Him. Sometimes I have prayed, "Lord, You have done such and such for this person in the Bible. And the Bible says that you don't show favoritism. I know I don't deserve all that You have already done for me, but I am your son and I am asking that You answer this prayer and help me in this situation." Many times, I have seen God answer that specific prayer, and I believe it is because He likes to see us exercise our faith.

Probably the most important thing I can say about fasting is that it needs to be done along with reading the Bible and praying. If we don't have the time to do this, then we are merely going hungry rather than receiving the benefits that come. Take the time that you would normally spend preparing a meal, cooking, and cleaning in order to use that time to get quiet before the Lord.

My typical fast is to go one day without food. I will drink water and coffee. This typically lasts from

Sunday night until Tuesday morning. During the day on Monday, I spend time in the Word and time worshipping while I am fasting. Then I will get up early on Tuesday and spend about one hour in a quiet room praying for breakthroughs from God. This is also a time to hear from God on decisions I am trying to make. I always have my Bible open because this is often how God speaks to me. It is truly amazing to me how we can find answers to today's problems by reading the Bible that was written two thousand years ago. Remember, it is the living Word of God!

I also can tell a difference in my focus when I am fasting. I don't know if it because my body is not working so hard to digest food in my stomach, but I do know that my mind seems clearer during this time.

I can tell you that I have seen tremendous things happen in my life, and much of it is due to regular fasting. This is a habit that I have now been doing for over thirty years, and I will continue it as long as I am able. Paul said that we are to *"present our bodies a living sacrifice" (Romans 12:1)*. What better way to do this than to starve our flesh and feed our spirit so we can get closer to God?

I hope that this chapter has helped you see the tremendous value that comes from fasting. I believe that if you will just try it for a short period of time, you will begin to reap some benefits and hopefully make it a part of your habits going forward.

Next, we will talk about the most mentioned topic in the Bible: finances.

4

Habit Number Four
Giving

"What shall I return to the Lord for all His goodness to me?" (Psalm 116:12 NIV)

You may ask why I put giving as a habit. I do this because giving needs to come as naturally as a habit to us. Money and possessions are two of the most talked about subjects in the entire Bible. As a matter of fact, according to Robert Morris, pastor of Gateway Church in Southlake Texas and author of *The Blessed Life*, "There are more than 500 verses in the Bible concerning prayer and nearly 500 verses concerning faith, but more than 2000 verses on the subject of money and possessions. Jesus talked about money in 16 of His 38 parables."

Why does the Bible put such an emphasis on money and possessions? I believe it is because we need to keep things in perspective and make sure that God is always first in our lives. When we spend most of our waking hours working for a paycheck and the size of that paycheck determines the quality of life we can afford, it is easy to see where our priorities can drift away from God.

It is human nature to seek success in our lives, and we can see multiple Scriptures that tell us that God wants our success. But we must always remember that God wants our primary focus to be on Him, and He will take care of everything else. Jesus said that we should *"seek first His kingdom and His righteousness; and all these things shall be added to you" (Matthew 6:33)*. "These things" are our food, clothing, and shelter. Jesus knew that these would always be concerns for us, and it is actually okay for us to desire those things, but we must always put Him first in whatever we do.

God knows that we have needs and we have desires. He wants to meet those for us so long as they are not going to harm us or become too important. You have probably heard it said that "God doesn't care if you have stuff, He just cares if your stuff has you." We all know people who put too much emphasis on their stuff and on "keeping up with the Joneses." Everyone knows people who seem to have a ton of stuff, but they seem miserable. It doesn't have to be that way!

If you have children, you know how much you desire for them to have what they need in life. I believe that God gave us this love for our kids so that we can get a glimpse of the love He has for us. Again, I mention the great verse that explains this in Matthew. *"If you then, being evil, know how to give good gifts to your children, how much more will your Father who is in heaven give what is good to those who ask Him!" (Matthew 7:11)*. This tells me that God loves me even more than I love my children, and He wants me to have success in my life; He just wants success to have its proper place.

Tony Dungy was the coach of the Indianapolis Colts and won the Super Bowl in 2006. He also set an NFL record for consecutive playoff appearances by a head coach in 2008 with ten straight appearances. He was then inducted into the Pro Football Hall of Fame in 2016. In other words, he has achieved success at the highest level in his profession. Even with all his success, he knows how to keep it in perspective. In his book *Uncommon,* he says that "God calls us to be faithful, not successful."

Being faithful is important in many areas. Being faithful in your job, being faithful to your spouse, and being faithful with your money are three areas emphasized in the Bible. The key is to keep the focus on pleasing God first; then the success that God wants us to have can be achieved and used for His purposes.

As we begin to explore what the Bible says about giving, it is good to understand that money is not good or bad. It is neutral. If you give money to a good person, he will do good things with it. Give money to a bad person and he will likely do bad things with it. Money can be used for good or for evil, but it is not good or evil by itself. And money is not the root of all evil! It is the *love* of money that is the root of all evil (1 Timothy 6:10). Obviously, this is not a new problem in society; as the Bible shows, society has struggled with love of money for thousands of years.

Everyone has read the parable of the sower and the seeds. This is one of the most important parables to understand. When asked to explain this parable, Jesus said to His disciples, *"Don't you understand this parable? How then will you understand any parable?"* *(Mark 4:13 NIV)*. Jesus is saying that it will be hard to understand any parable if we don't understand this one, so it is important that we figure this one out.

Jesus said the seed was the Word. Some of the seed fell by the road and was eaten by birds. Some fell on the rocks and didn't last because there were no roots. Then some fell among thorns and the thorns choked the seed as it grew. He explained that this seed represented the people who heard the word and received it, but then *"the worries of the world, the deceitfulness of riches, and the desires for other things enter in and choke the word and it becomes unfruitful"* *(Mark 4:19)*.

In other words, Jesus says that many will hear the message of the gospel and receive it. But they will allow the desire for riches and things to choke the word out of their lives so that they can bear no fruit. He goes on to say that the seeds sown on the good soil were the people who hear the word and accept it, and then bear fruit, *"thirty, sixty, and a hundredfold"* *(Mark 4:20)*.

We can all say that we want to be the people who bear fruit for the kingdom, so we must guard our heart against every form of greed and desire for riches. The best way I know to do that is to have a proper understanding of money and its use.

As we go through this chapter, we will discuss why we should give our money, how we should give, how much we should give, and the many benefits that accompany giving. We will also discuss whether we are allowed to enjoy our possessions and whether our money and possessions are all we should give. Hopefully, by the end of this chapter you will have a much clearer understanding of the Bible's perspective on money.

Why should we give?

The simple and easy answer is, again, because Jesus said to give. Remember in one of His very first sermons, He said, "When you give..., when you pray..., when you fast..."? He did not say "if" we do these three things, but "when" we do them. So evidently the people listening to Him were to understand that this was a normal part of living our Christian life.

This theme is repeated throughout the Bible. Psalms says, *"the godly are generous givers" (Psalms 37:21 NLT)*. And in Proverbs, we read that the *"godly love to give" (Proverbs 21:26 NLT)*. And then Paul exhorted us in 2 Corinthians to *"excel in [our] giving" (2 Corinthians 8:7 NLT)*. The bottom line is this: no amount of giving is too generous for God. He Himself gave us more than we can ever repay when He sent Jesus. *"What shall I return to the Lord for all His goodness to me?" (Psalm 116:12 NIV)*.

It seems more natural to give when we consider what God has given to us. Consider the story in Luke 7 about the woman who came to the Pharisee's house where Jesus was dining. She put oil on His feet, wet them with her tears, and then wiped them with her hair. The Pharisee thought that Jesus would not have allowed her to touch Him if He had known what kind of sinner the woman was. Jesus, aware of the man's thoughts, told him that people who are forgiven much love much. I think about this often because I know that I have been forgiven much from my past, and that gives me the desire to give back to God for what He has done for me.

One of the ways to do that is to find people who are hurting, or are less fortunate, and give them what they need. Jesus said that even one who gives a cold drink of water to one of the least will be rewarded in heaven. Those are the rewards we should all be seeking!

We must also have a proper perspective on money and realize that it is really not ours. We are merely managers of what all belongs to God. Back in the Old Testament, we can see that all money comes from God:

> *"Wealth and honor come from You; You are the ruler of all things. In Your hands are strength and power to exalt and give strength to all. Now, our God, we give You thanks, and praise Your glorious name. But who am I, and who are my people, that we should be able to give as generously as this? Everything comes from You, and we have given You only what comes from Your hand"* (1 Chronicles 29:12-14 NIV).

In other words, all money and wealth come from God. We are merely stewards of what He has given us on this earth. We are not owners, but managers. The day will come when we will stand before Him and give an account of what we did with everything He gave to us. Our money, our wealth, our time, our talents, everything. The Bible tells us, *"The earth is the Lord's,*

and all it contains, the world, and those who dwell in it"
(Psalm 24:1).

I love how Andy Stanley explains this in his book
How to be Rich:

> "God doesn't want to take your money; He
> just doesn't want your money to take you.
> First of all, He doesn't need your permis-
> sion to take your stuff. It's already His any-
> way. Second, God is a giver, not a taker. He
> didn't send His son, Jesus, to collect from
> everyone who owed Him. He sent Jesus
> to give His life for you and by calling you
> to acknowledge Him as the owner of your
> stuff, He wants to give you something yet
> again. He wants to give you the freedom
> and peace that come with letting go."

Think of it like this. If I let someone stay in my
house when I am gone, I expect it to be in good
shape when I come home. It is still my house; I
simply allowed them to enjoy it while I was away.
I would hope they would respect my things and
not tear anything up because it is not theirs- it is
mine. In the same way, God has entrusted us to
live on this earth and to enjoy it, but it is His. He
wants us to be good stewards while we are here.
God wants us to enjoy it, but we must remember
it is all His, including all the money. When we

have this perspective, it is easier to look at money as a way to fulfill whatever He has called us to do.

When God placed Adam and Eve in the Garden of Eden, He appointed them as stewards and told them to work the garden and enjoy everything that was there. He just told them to leave the one tree alone. When they disobeyed God and ate from that tree, they acted as if they were the owners of the garden rather than just stewards of it. It was because of this disobedience that they were sent away from the garden.

We should give because the Bible says so. This entire book is based on how to live the abundant life that God wants us to have. We have seen that this success can only come when we are obedient. Now we know God wants us to give because it is all His anyway, so obeying God by giving is one way to help achieve the abundant life. Now let's discuss how much we should give.

How much should we give?

There is no set amount that each of us must give of our possessions. But the Bible gives some clarity about certain aspects of giving. For example, tithing is discussed throughout the Bible all the way back in Genesis, when Abraham gave a tenth of his possessions to Melchizedek. I believe that, as a minimum, believers need to give ten percent of their money to the local church where they are being fed spiritually. Before you tune out because your budget is way too tight to start giving ten percent, please bear with me and read the rest of this chapter. You will be amazed at what can happen when you simply obey God in this one area of your life!

A good question you may be asking is that if God doesn't need our money because He already owns the entire world, then why does He want us to return ten percent of our money to the local church? I believe there are several answers. First, He wants our obedience more than anything. Also, tithing exercises our faith. The Bible tells us that *"without faith, it is impossible to please God" (Hebrews 11:6)*. For us to let go of ten percent of our money, we must use real faith to believe that God can use the other ninety percent to pay all of our bills. Tithing also helps keep us from getting snared by the deceitfulness of riches, which is what keep many from following God (as illustrated in the parable of the sower). Just remember that 90% of our income with the blessing of God goes a lot farther than 100% without His blessing.

Why do you think God asks us to give a tenth? Here is what Robert Morris says in *The Blessed Life*:

> "The word translated 'tithe' in the Bible means 'tenth' or a 'tenth part.' And you know what the number 10 represents all through the Bible? It represents testing. Let me give you a few examples. How many plagues were there in Egypt? How many commandments are there? How many times did God test Jacob's heart when he was working for Laban? How many days was Daniel tested in the first chapter of the book of Daniel? In Matthew 25, 10 virgins had their preparedness tested. 10 days of testing are mentioned in Revelation 2:10. What is true is that the number 10 is associated with testing throughout the Bible. And the tithe represents the ultimate 'heart test' for the believer. But, more specifically, tithing is also the only area in which the Christian is invited to test God."

It is always easiest if you start tithing from the first job you ever get, but that is not often the case. Over the years of being a Christian, I have met with many people who have seen in the Bible that God wants us to tithe and have started giving for the first time. Because they couldn't start with a full ten percent,

117

they worked up to that amount by giving what they could at first and then giving more. Many times, this meant cutting back in other areas of their lives. I have seen people trade their car for a cheaper car just so they could begin obeying God in this important area of their lives.

There are many good budgeting books out there to help with this when money seems tight. I would recommend looking on Amazon or going to the bookstore if you need help in this area. Just know that all the people I have ever seen commit to changing their budget so they could tithe ten percent never regretted doing it. There are many benefits to this that we will discuss later in more detail, but a concept to understand now is that God can do more with your budget with ninety percent than you can do by yourself with one hundred percent. We should always strive to have God working on our behalf, and the Bible is full of promises that He will do just that when we are obedient with our giving.

One of the richest men who ever lived, John D. Rockefeller, was said to have tithed from an early age. According to Charles Stanley in *Success God's Way*,

> "John D Rockefeller once said, 'I never would have been able to tithe on my first million dollars if I had not learned to tithe on my first paycheck, which was $1.50 for

the week.' John D Rockefeller had a godly
attitude toward money. He was perhaps
the most generous philanthropist the
United States has ever seen. And he also
became one of the wealthiest men ever to
live in America."

The Bible also tells us that the tithe should come from
all of our increase. In Leviticus we read, *"Thus all the
tithe of the land, of the seed of the land or of the fruit of
the tree, is the Lord's; it is holy to the Lord" (Leviticus
27:30)*. In other words, the way I read this, anything
that we receive as far as money, or wealth, should be
tithed to the church.

Once we have established the habit of tithing, we
should also start the habit of setting aside some
money for offerings. We should make it a priority to
always have some money around for a need when it
arises. Again, this will probably mean changing some
financial habits so we can get to this point, but it is all
about obeying God so we can have the true abundant
life He wants us to experience.

As we think about giving offerings above our tithe,
it is good to remember that Paul told us *"not to give
under compulsion" (2 Corinthians 9:7)*. I recently met
with a young couple who wanted my opinion on giving to help fund construction of a new building for
their church. They were new to this church, and when

they met with the pastor in a new member's class, he told them the church had started construction but did not have enough money to finish. The pastor wanted each person to give a certain amount by the end of the year. He even told the couple the amount to give! The couple felt awkward about this and wanted my opinion. I told them that I believed this type of situation is why Paul wrote 2 Corinthians 9:7, exhorting us not to give under compulsion.

Using business principles, I want my giving to have a good return on it. Bankers refer to this as an ROI, or return on investment. I believe God is pleased when we look at our giving this way. The best return that I want to get is people getting to know God in a real way. Sometimes a new church building can help reach that goal, but it is important to seek wisdom from God and let Him lead you instead of allowing yourself to be motivated by guilt.

I have given to church building campaigns over the years and want to share a very personal story of one time in particular. I was very involved in this particular church, and its leaders wanted to construct a very nice building in a prime location. This building would help the church grow because of where it was located. I had been an active member of the church and had given a significant amount of money in a prior campaign. Because of this, the pastor had asked me to serve on the campaign to help raise the money. We had set a date for giving our pledge, which would be paid over three years, and the date was getting closer without me having a clear direction on what to do. I had recently sold my business and was in the process of building a new business, and there wasn't much income yet. I had a wife and two young daughters at home.

I am sure you get the picture- I did not have much extra money sitting around and it would have been much easier to just sit this one out. Actually, because of my financial situation, I believe the pastor would have totally understood. I felt no pressure to do something that wasn't wise, but I really did want to help in a meaningful way, as I had always been a big contributor. My wife was also praying and seeking direction so that we would be on the same page.

One night I was exercising on an elliptical machine and just praying to God. I told Him that I really needed some direction on what to do. I had a number in my mind that was equivalent to the previous pledge I had made several years earlier, and I simply asked God if this was the number. I felt Him say "No," so I doubled the number and asked again. Again, I felt Him say "No." So I doubled the number a second time and asked if this was the number and I felt God say, "Yes!"

I have to admit that this was a little bit scary. My girls were both young, and this amount of money was more than I was making in an entire year! I reminded God (not that He needed it) that my business was not taking off yet and I needed to be sure this was what He wanted me to do. I felt God tell me that if I would trust in Him, He would do amazing things in my business. Let me be clear: I did not look at giving to my church because of something I thought God would do in return. I just wanted to obey what I felt He had told me.

Because of the amount of this pledge, I told God that if this was truly Him speaking this, I needed Him to speak the same amount to my wife Lucy. The amazing thing about my marriage is that we both have a gift of giving and both believe we can hear from God. I went downstairs and told Lucy that I really needed her to pray and get an answer. She told me that she had already heard an answer, but wasn't sure it was from God because it was too much. She not only paid our household bills, but she worked in my company and knew very precisely where our finances were.

I asked her what her number was, and she told me the exact number that I had felt God tell me! This whole process may sound crazy to you, but this is how this has worked out for me over the years- by just having simple faith and believing that God wants to direct all of my paths. Lucy and I both agreed with excitement that this must be the Lord and that we would make the pledge.

This was to be a three-year pledge and we were able to pay it off in less than two years! On top of that, my business started growing at an incredible pace and we were honored to be placed on the prestigious INC 500 list three years in a row. This annual list identifies the 500 fastest growing companies in America and is a very prestigious recognition to get even one time. We were recognized for three straight years!

I can honestly say that this had less to do with me and my business skills and much more to do with a God who rewards obedience. I did not seek rewards from God, but I have realized from many years of living this way that God does reward those who seek Him.

The key from this section is not to get hung up on the amount of money to give, but to learn to be obedient and give when God moves us to do so. And it starts with the tithe, which is discussed throughout the Bible. Giving ten percent of your money is simply obeying God in something He has already said to do.

Now let's discuss some practical ideas on giving.

How should we give?

One of the keys of giving I see throughout the Bible is that it should always be from the first. God does not want to take second place in our lives to anything, including money. In His very first commandment to Moses, God said He was a jealous God and wants us to have no other gods before Him. These gods can be anything: possessions, people, careers, money, or even food. God wants to be first.

In Romans, we see that we are saved when we *"confess with our mouths that Jesus is Lord and believe in our heart that God raised Him from the dead" (Romans 10:9)*. For Jesus to be Lord of our lives, He must be first in everything.

Tithing is a way for us to show God that He is first.

> *"You must tithe all of your crops every year. Bring this tithe to eat before the Lord your God at the place he shall choose as his sanctuary; this applies to your tithes of grain, new wine, olive oil, and the firstborn of your flocks and herds. The purpose of tithing is to teach you always to put God first in your lives" (Deuteronomy 14:22-23 TLB).*

Have you ever wondered in the story of Cain and Abel in Genesis 4 why God said He had regard for Abel and his offering but had no regard for Cain and his offering? Why would this be, when they both brought their offering to the Lord? When you look closely, you see that Cain brought his offering from the fruit of the ground, but Abel brought his from the firstborn of his flock:

> *"Now Abel kept flocks, and Cain worked the soil. In the course of time Cain brought some of the fruits of the soil as an offering to the Lord. And Abel also brought an offering—fat portions from some of the firstborn of his flock. The Lord looked with favor on Abel and his offering, but on Cain and his offering he did not look with favor. So Cain was very angry, and his face was downcast" (Genesis 4:2-5 NIV).*

We see in this passage that God had regard for Abel's offering because he brought it from the first of his possessions.

We read again in Exodus 23 that, when Moses is giving instruction to Israel on how to live, he tells them to bring the *"choice first fruits of your soil into the house of the Lord your God" (Exodus 23:19).* And then *Proverbs 3:9* says to *"honor the Lord from your wealth, and from the first of all your produce."*

This is a good place to answer the question, should we give from our gross income, or our net income? I have been asked this several times and believe the Bible is quite clear: God wants to be first in our lives, and He wants to receive from the first of *all* of our gains- financial and otherwise. Again, it isn't because God needs our money. God does not need our money. He just wants our obedience so that He can use us to further His kingdom on this earth. He wants to break us from the desire for riches, which will never satisfy. We show our obedience to His instruction by learning to give what is already His.

God also tells us that we should pass this idea of tithing down to our children so they will understand it:

> *"And it shall be when your son asks you in time to come, saying, 'What is this?' then you shall say to him, 'With a powerful hand the Lord brought us out of Egypt, from the house of slavery. It came about, when Pharaoh was stubborn about letting us go, that the Lord killed every firstborn in the land of Egypt, both the firstborn of man and the firstborn of beast. Therefore, I sacrifice to the Lord the males, the first offspring of every womb, but every firstborn of my sons I redeem'"* (Exodus 13:14–15).

We are to sit our children down and tell them that, before we were Christians, we were enslaved to our sin, but God came and set us free; that is why we now give back the first of everything we produce. We don't give it because we consider it a debt we owe, but because we love God for what He has done for us and we are being obedient to His Word.

This is one of the most important principles I taught my girls, and they have been tithing ever since they started their jobs as teenagers. Now that they are adults and have careers, it is much easier to continue because they learned to give from the first and then use what is left for their bills and savings. This is so much easier when you start this habit at a young age, which is why I believe we are encouraged to sit our children down and explain it to them early on. If they take hold of this concept in their heart and make it a habit from an early age, they will be better prepared to live on the ninety percent that is left.

So what does it look like to give from the first of our produce? I believe it looks like paying our tithe before we pay any of our other bills: before the mortgage, before the car payment, before food and clothing. If we get paid on the first day of the month, or the tenth day of the month, or every Friday, we should simply pay our tithe before anything else gets paid. This is much easier to do today with the ease of online giving. I have been doing this practice for many years of bringing my tithe first to the church, before anything else, and I can tell you that it works.

Another point I want to make regarding how we should give is that it should be done in secret. We don't give to receive any recognition from men, or to be seen as more spiritual than someone who doesn't give. We are simply being obedient. Remember that Jesus told us not to pray, fast, or give to be seen by men, because if we do, that will be our reward in full (Matthew 6:2). Instead, we should pray, fast, and give in secret, and the God who sees in secret will repay us.

In his book *A Life God Rewards*, Bruce Wilkinson shares the teachings of Charles H. Spurgeon:

> "Seek secrecy for your good deeds. Do not even see your own virtue. Hide from yourself that which you yourself have done that is commendable; for the proud contemplation of your own generosity may tarnish all your alms. Keep the thing so secret that even you yourself are hardly aware that you are doing anything at all praiseworthy. Let God be present, and you will have enough of an audience. He will reward you, reward you openly, reward you as a father rewards a child, reward you as one who saw what you did, and knew that you did it wholly unto Him."

Now that we understand that God wants us to tithe, let's look at some of the benefits that come from giving.

Benefits of Giving

The Bible clearly states benefits that come from our giving. I want to be very clear that I don't think we should seek anything from God for our giving. We are simply being obedient, a common theme for an abundant life. For us to receive the abundant life Jesus has for us, we must be obedient. I see nothing in the Bible that says our motive should be personal gain. There are many people who lead people astray with a "name it and claim it" gospel, but I want no part of that. We should never give to get; we can give, to get, to give again! Our goal should be to act as a conduit through which God gives so we can bless others with it. When He sees that this is our heart's intention, He will allow the giving to flow through us.

❖ It rebukes the enemy

One of my favorite verses on giving comes from the last book of the Old Testament, Malachi. I read it as a college student and I just decided I was going to believe it. Like with fasting, I was not told about tithing very much as a young person. My parents both tithed, but they didn't really talk about it with the kids. So, when I read my Bible in college, much of this was new to me. I read in Malachi where God says we can actually test Him with our giving. If we bring the whole tithe into the storehouse- the local church that is feeding us spiritually- then *"God will rebuke the devourer for you, so that it may not destroy the fruits of the ground; nor will the vine in the field cast its grapes"* (*Malachi 3:11*).

There is more to this passage that I will share soon, but I believe strongly that there is an enemy out there who is trying to destroy us. He does not want our Christianity to work; if he can keep us away from the promises of God through any means, then he will. I also think the enemy knows our weaknesses, and he will attack us in those areas- whether it is money, or people, or things. But, there is good news! As we see here in the Bible, God clearly says there is a way for us to protect ourselves financially: by bringing the entire tithe into the storehouse.

I also love the fact He says we can test Him in this. I began this "test" by tithing as a new Christian with very limited money, and have continued throughout my thirty-five years of being a Christian. I can say emphatically that it works.

Many years ago, I was sitting in a business conference with a good pastor friend of mine, Herb Eplee. There were a couple dozen people in the room, and Herb made the comment to me that everyone in the room was tithing on their income. I told him he was wrong because I knew everyone in the room, and many of them didn't even go to church. He responded that people who do not tithe to their local church spend their money on repair bills and things that break or wear out before they should. He explained that the devourer was working in everyone's life who did not have the protection of God. After observing this for many years now, I must say that I agree with him.

It may sound crazy to you, but things just do not wear out easily at my house. I just replaced a clothes dryer that Lucy and I received when we got married thirty-three years ago. And it was used when we got it! The machine was still working with no issues when we replaced it- we just decided it was time for a new one. And I could talk about cars, clothes, and other things that just seem to last longer.

Over the years, we would save our money and buy used vehicles for cash instead of going into debt on new vehicles. This was in spite of the fact that we both had college degrees and well-paying jobs. We just believed that if we were disciplined with our money and paid tithes and offerings first, God would allow the vehicles to last longer- and they did. To this day we continue to pay cash for every vehicle we buy (thankfully they are a little nicer than the cars we started out with!).

I have also had many instances where I have gotten unusual deals on certain purchases. Take, for example, the boat I bought when my girls started college several years ago. We invested in a lake house and a boat so that the girls could take their friends there instead of the college party scene. Boats can be tricky though, because they depreciate so quickly. If you own a boat or know someone who does, you may know the joke: the two happiest days for a boat owner are the day they bought it and the day they sold it. That was not the case for me.

I purchased the boat at a boat show. I am careful with my money on all purchases, especially large ones, because I know I am simply a steward of the money for a short time. At this show, I went around and negotiated between different companies for quite some time before settling on the exact boat. We bought the boat and used it happily while the girls were in college. Then, once both girls had graduated, gotten married, and moved out of state to begin their careers, we didn't have the need for the boat anymore. I called the marina where I bought it and asked what the selling price would be. The guy looked it up and gave me a number. Then I asked him to look up what I paid for it because I couldn't remember. He laughed when he told me the amount because it was within five hundred dollars of the present value! He said I actually paid less than their cost for the boat and was surprised at the deal I had gotten over five years ago. I just see this as another way God takes care of my finances because I am faithful with what He has given me.

Let me share another personal story that showed me how God takes care of us as we are faithful. Being in the construction business was extremely difficult during the recession that started for us in the fall of 2008. The recession started in some areas of the country before that, but it was all from the same source- reckless lending practices by banks. (I am not trying to place any blame, but it was honestly shocking to see how people with no jobs could purchase a house leading up to this crisis. Common sense would tell you this was not sustainable!) When the crisis came, it came hard. Many really good people were put out of business. Some business people even committed suicide in our city because the stress of trying to work out of the mess was too much to handle. Needless to say, this was a tough time for all of us in the industry, me included.

I was probably about three years into working through everything. I would work basically from six in the morning until after midnight, just trying to scratch my way out. I had many people counting on me to make it. The easy road would have been to follow many of my peers by declaring bankruptcy, but I just felt that I had made commitments to the banks and I needed to find a way to honor those commitments. Many nights around midnight, I would sit outside and just talk to God, searching for ideas and answers. One night, I felt the pressure was overwhelming me. I told God I was desperate, and I needed His help.

At the time, it had been three years since either Lucy or I had taken a paycheck. It was critical that we kept paying our people, so we cashed all our savings in and sold everything we could to survive. That night when I was so desperate, I felt God tell me He wanted me to start tithing again. I said out loud to Him that I had nothing to tithe on because I wasn't making any money and had not been making money for three years. I felt God tell me again that He wanted me to tithe the amount I was tithing when I had a paycheck. I was so desperate that I was willing to try anything, and it was one of those times when I felt confident God was speaking.

The next morning, I told Lucy about my conversation and what I believed God had told me to do. Her first question was "Where is the money going to come from?" I told her I didn't know yet, and that God would have to provide it. Being the great wife that she is, Lucy agreed and began sending our tithe in as if we were receiving a paycheck. I cannot say this was easy, or that our financial picture changed overnight, but what I do know is that we paid back every single dollar to the banks and miraculously were able to pay all of our people on time every week.

I have had numerous banks ask me how in the world I survived this when so many others didn't. One of the big banks in town was serving six hundred builders at the beginning of the recession, and by the end of it, it was only loaning to three. I was one of the three! When I am asked this question, I typically give an answer that they may understand, like I paid everyone on time and stayed in touch with all of the banks. But the reality was that God had told me to do something very bold, and I obeyed Him. I attribute the fact that my business survived to my obedience with tithing during that impossible season. An even crazier fact is that my business is over two times the size it was before the recession, and growing! Obeying God really does work!

❖ Receive rewards in heaven

Another benefit I see clearly from Scripture is that, when we give our money for kingdom purposes, we are storing up treasures in heaven. Paul told Timothy to command the rich to *"do good, to be rich in good deeds, and to be generous and willing to share. In this way they will lay up treasure for themselves as a firm foundation for the coming age, so that they may take hold of the life that is truly life"* (1 Timothy 6:18-19).

Or, as Dwight Nichols says in *God's Plan for Your Finances*, "The only thing that will count for eternity is what we have done for the kingdom of God - how we have used the resources that God has provided to benefit the kingdom."

I believe firmly that our tithe, or first ten percent, must go to the local church, as stated in Malachi. The Bible tells us to give above and beyond our tithes with offerings outside of the ten percent, and we can see in the Scriptures there is flexibility on where this extra money goes. My personal conviction is that I want a good return on the money I give. If I am told to share my resources and, in doing so, I am laying up treasures in heaven, then I want my money to be used for the best possible return. In other words, I want my offerings to make an eternal impact on someone's life. That is the best kind of reward!

I see many ways to create this return with my giving. Church plants, or new churches, are one of the primary ways for people to become Christians, so investing in that is usually a great idea. I also see many foreign opportunities, where our money can be stretched much further than it can in America. The biggest filter that I use is to find out how many people are hearing the gospel and coming into a relationship with God. The Bible is very clear that God's passion is for the lost sheep, so that is where I want my resources to be focused.

I love how Robert Morris says it in *The Blessed Life*:

"If I use my money to bring people to Christ, they will welcome me into heaven when I die. Use your money to affect people – to help them hear the gospel – and they will form part of your welcoming committee when you get to heaven."

Remember that the Bible says we are not saved *by* our works, but we are saved *for* good works. God even prepared these works for us beforehand! *"For we are His workmanship, created in Christ Jesus for good works, which God prepared beforehand so that we would walk in them" (Ephesians 2:10)*. Essentially, God chose us to be a part of His kingdom so that we will do good works. But did you know the Bible also says there are rewards for these good works? Jesus said, *"For whoever gives you a cup of water to drink because of your name as followers of Christ, truly I say to you, he will not lose his reward" (Mark 9:41)*.

Jesus is saying that if we do anything to help those who are doing His work, even in as small a thing as giving a cup of water, we will be rewarded. We should constantly be looking for ways to be a blessing to those around us, especially those who are believers. This is why I also love to invest my money in young people going on mission trips. I have helped many people go overseas to share the gospel or help build a church. These trips have an eternal impact on people in these places, as well as an impact on those who go. I know the impact my mission trip to the Philippines had on me the summer I graduated college. It is hard to go to third-world countries and not be impacted for life. It gives a true perspective of how blessed we are in this country. We need to remember that those blessings come so we can help others. What we do with our money and resources does matter.

In *How to be Rich*, Andy Stanley puts it another way: "On this point Jesus could not be clearer. It's not what you have that matters. It's what you do with what you have that will count either for you or against you in the kingdom of heaven." God does not mind us having money; He just wants us to keep it in perspective. Instead of viewing our money only as a way to meet our needs and fulfill our desires, we need to see our money also as a way to plant seeds that will bear fruit for eternity.

It is easy to see that rewards will come for us in heaven as we are faithful in giving to others, but what about rewards on earth? I believe the Bible is also clear about this.

❖ God will repay us here on earth

We should never give our money simply so that we can get something in return from God. But we cannot ignore what the Bible clearly says on this subject. I believe God includes these promises to comfort us in knowing that He will repay us for our good deeds.

"Give, and it will be given to you. A good measure, pressed down, shaken together and running over, will be poured into your lap. For with the measure you use, it will be measured to you" (Luke 6:38 NIV). The King James Version says, *"Men will pour into your bosom."* This doesn't sound like a reward we will receive in heaven, but on earth. There are rewards for our faithfulness here on earth.

The Bible also says that we will be repaid with the same measure that we give. This tells me that if I give a thimble full of something away, I will receive a thimble full back. If I give a cup full, then I will receive a cup full back. But if I use a bucket to give, then God will repay me with buckets. God doesn't want us to just rely on good luck to get by. His system is quite different. As Fred Price says in *The Purpose of Prosperity*, "God does not rely on any lotto to get money to you. His method is sowing and reaping, and paying tithes and giving offerings. If you do that, the Lord will bless you, and cause you to be a blessing to others."

It isn't always just money we receive when we give. Oftentimes we receive back whatever it is that we give. Peter said to Jesus, "Behold, we have left everything and followed You." Jesus said:

> *"Truly I say to you, there is no one who has left house or brothers or sisters or mother or father or children or farms, for My sake and for the gospel's sake, but that he will receive a hundred times as much now in the present age, houses and brothers and sisters and mothers and children and farms, along with persecutions; and in the age to come, eternal life" (Mark 10:28-30).*

This passage has always meant a lot to me because, when I became a Christian, I felt I had to not only drastically change my lifestyle, but I also needed to change my companions. Unfortunately for me, this meant I had to separate myself from my brothers. As hard as that was, I knew it was the only way I would be successful in following God, since my brothers wanted me to continue living a partying lifestyle with them. I remember my mom struggling to understand why I didn't want to come home as much and hang out. As painful as it was, I knew it was the right thing to do. Now, I look around me and see all the wonderful friends I have whom I consider brothers, and I know that God has been faithful to fulfill the promise that Jesus gave to Peter: we receive back whatever it is we give up.

If you look closely at the passage in Mark 10, you see that Jesus says we will receive back in this present age as well as the age to come. It is obvious that God does reward us here on earth for obeying His Word.

Remember when we read about the parable of the sower and the seed? Jesus asked His disciples how they could understand any of the parables if they didn't understand this one. This is why: God's whole economy is set up by sowing and reaping. He does not simply want us to hoard all of our money, or just save it for a rainy day. I do believe in saving for the future, but I also believe that having a proper perspective on our giving is ultimately more important. To put it another way, in his book *Trust God For Your Finances*, Jack Hartman says, "God doesn't multiply the seeds that we retain; he only multiplies the seeds we sow."

I want to reiterate again that I don't believe we should give just because of what we receive in return. But I can tell you that, by living this Christian life now for thirty-five years and always looking for opportunities to help others quietly with my money, I have seen amazing returns that can never be interpreted as just luck. I truly believe that God does reward us for doing good things with our money.

Other verses that confirm this include:

> *"Good will come to those who are generous and lend freely, who conduct their affairs with justice" (Psalm 112:5 NIV).*

> *"A generous person will prosper; who-*
> *ever refreshes others will be refreshed"*
> *(Proverbs 11:25 NIV).*

> *"One who is gracious to a poor man lends*
> *to the Lord, and He will repay him for*
> *his good deed" (Proverbs 19:17).*

> *"Honor the Lord from your wealth and*
> *from the first of all your produce; so*
> *your barns will be filled with plenty and*
> *your vats will overflow with new wine"*
> *(Proverbs 3:10).*

> *"I have been young and now I am old,*
> *yet I have not seen the righteous forsaken*
> *or his descendants begging bread. All*
> *day long he is gracious and lends, and*
> *his descendants are a blessing" (Psalm*
> *37:25-26).*

I know that all of us would like for our children to be blessed. If we are constantly looking for ways to be financial blessing to others, the Bible says our descendants will then be blessed. What a great promise!

Does God bless us financially so we look good to our friends? I believe not! I believe that God blesses us so that we can have more to give. Or, as Dave Ramsey says in *The Total Money Makeover*, "God tends to pour blessings on people going in a direction He wants them to go." As we are faithful with what God has entrusted to us, God will allow us to have more so we can continue being a blessing to others. This is how the love of God is shared with the world: through Christians looking for ways to bless others. And God will find that person and pour blessings on them to keep doing His work.

> *"And God is able to bless you abundantly, so that in all things at all times, having all that you need, you will abound in every good work"* (2 Corinthians 9:8 NIV).

> *"Now He who supplies seed to the sower and bread for food will also supply and increase your store of seed and will enlarge the harvest of your righteousness. You will be enriched in every way so that you can be generous on every occasion, and through us your generosity will result in thanksgiving to God"* (2 Corinthians 9:11 NIV).

This great passage tells us that, as we continue to give, God will give back to us to the point where we will always have enough to give for every good work. Wow, what a promise! Also note that it is God who gives us the seed to sow. In other words, God is watching how much we are willing to sow into His work, and then He gives back to us according to the same measure we are using. Think of a farmer who harvests his crop. The only way he will get another crop next season is for him to have more seed to sow. In the same way, God is the One who gives us the seed for the next harvest. This is an exciting concept!

Before moving on to another exciting benefit we get from our giving, I want to pause and share some simple wisdom. I have seen people hear this type of message and then go do something foolish, like give money they needed for their mortgage payment, and expect to have God bless that. That usually ends in frustration with God. If money is tight, which it is for most of us, then you must start with changing some priorities. If debt is a burden to the point that you don't see any way to give either a tithe or an offering, and your heart is willing to move forward in this area, then take a serious look at what you spend money on and see what adjustments can be made to your lifestyle.

There are many great authors and speakers who specialize on the subject of budgeting and money. I highly recommend Dave Ramsey if you need help in this area. I won't spend much time on this other than to say that I have seen countless young couples over the years who saw no light in their finances, so they made changes to their lifestyles in order to begin tithing; and God worked miracles in their lives. This doesn't always happen quickly, but our God is faithful! He is looking for our obedience, and obeying Him with our giving is necessary if we want to see all He has in store for us and to reap the abundant life Jesus promised.

I wish I had the time to share all the stories of couples I know who have sold a car, or downsized a house, and started living below their means so they could give more easily. In almost all cases, when someone has made this commitment, in a matter of time their finances improved. It doesn't make any sense in the natural mind to think that we can actually live better on ninety percent of our money while giving ten percent to God than we could by living on the full one-hundred percent. But trust me that it works! And when God sees us working hard to turn the financial corner, He gets involved in making things happen in our favor.

The best part of me saying this about money is that I am not a pastor asking for your money! I am simply a businessman who put these principles to the test, and I am living proof that it works. If you are sensing a desire to try this, there is a good chance it is the Holy Spirit touching your heart so that the blessings of God can become real in your life. I challenge you to give it a try!

❖ We fulfill the promise of Abraham, to be a blessing

A final benefit is that, by giving our money, we can fulfill the promise God made to Abraham and his offspring: that we would be blessed so that we could be a blessing. Genesis 12 says that all the families of the earth will be blessed through Abraham. As we discussed in chapter two, we saw in both Galatians and Hebrews that, as believers in Jesus, we are the offspring of Abraham and heirs to the same promise God made to him. This promise is that God would surely bless us and surely multiply us. I believe this comes to us in full as we are looking around for ways to be a blessing to others.

In *How to be Rich*, Andy Stanley says, "You miss money you misspend. You miss money you waste or poorly invest. But you never miss money given to meet a need in someone's life. Put another way, we become discontented with ourselves when we mishandle our money, but we find contentment through responsible generosity." Everyone knows the feeling of giving money to someone who truly has a need and making a difference for them. It is a great feeling when we are able to see the need and fulfill it. Don't you think God is looking for the humble person who is constantly on the lookout for those types of opportunities?

Let me share stories of two young men that my family has had the opportunity to bless. I share these simply to inspire you to be on the lookout for similar opportunities.

Before my twin daughters went off to college, I had a good friend and mentor, Bob Weiner, come with his wife, Rose, and spend a day praying over my girls and preparing them for college. Bob has spent decades planting churches all over the world, and he has seen thousands of people changed because of his ministry. Both my wife and I are Christians because Bob planted a small church in our college town in the late 1970's that reached out to college students.

One of Bob's primary objectives is to reach the international students who are here on our campuses. There are many Scriptures that tell us to help and look after the foreigners in our land. See *Leviticus 19:34 (NIV): "The foreigner residing among you must be treated as your native-born. Love them as yourself, for you were foreigners in Egypt. I am the LORD your God."* Another reason is that these students are usually here because they are among the best and brightest from their countries, and can go home and make a huge impact for Christ.

Many times, when these elite students come to our college campuses, they have their first experience being around Christians. Bob and Rose spent time explaining this to my girls and giving them a vision for reaching these international students. Just a few short weeks after this, my daughter Melissa met a man coming out of a store and she felt God urging her to speak to him. She said "hello," and when he responded she noticed he had an accent, so they started a conversation. Melissa called me just after this encounter because she wanted me to drive two hours that Sunday and go with them to church.

When I met Eric Kokoye that weekend, I had no idea of the impact that simple meeting outside the store would have. Eric's story is amazing. He grew up in the small country of Benin, Africa. He was the first person in his family to go to college. When he graduated, he went to Germany to get a Master's degree. During his three years there, nobody befriended him or even welcomed him in their home. When he graduated with his Master's degree, he applied for a PhD at Auburn University in Agricultural Economics since he had heard that Auburn had a good agricultural program. He was accepted and was to receive a work fellowship so that he could afford to live and go to school. When Melissa met him, he was at a low point in his life. His Visa was held up, so he could not work, and he was running out of money. To top it off, he had taken his first test and failed it. Later, he told me that he had gone and sat under a tree and prayed that if God was real and would help him, he would serve God for the rest of his life. He met Melissa within a couple days.

Shortly after meeting Eric, we invited him to our lake house to get to know him better. My wife and I both know that these "chance" meetings with people are often orchestrated by God, so we wanted to hear his story. As he began to tell us his situation, Lucy and I looked at each other and knew this wasn't just a coincidence, but that we were supposed to help him. Because he was out of money and had nothing to eat, we went to the bank and got him some money for food. As we left the bank, Eric had tears in his eyes. I asked him what was wrong, and he simply said, "God is good!" We also helped with rent and other expenses until his Visa was approved and he could begin to work.

At this time, Eric had not seen his mother for over four years. He had been sending money home from his meager pay in Germany so that his cousin could build a house for his mother. She had never had her own home. When Eric was telling me this, I asked him the total amount the house would cost. He told me it was $5,000. What a small amount for a house! He had been sacrificing for four years to see her simple dream come true. We helped finish the house and then sent Eric home to Benin that Christmas so that he could spend time with his mom in her new home.

The next year Eric met and married a beautiful lady named Renee, also from Benin. They had their first child, a son- and named him Glenn! He will grow up with me as his grandfather! What an honor. We sent Eric's mom on her first plane ride to come stay for a few months and help with the baby. It was such a pleasure to meet her. When I asked her what it was like having Eric here with no money, and her not being able to help him, she said that she was just praying that God would make Himself real to Eric. I believe that prayer has been answered!

Eric is now working very successfully at a bank in Arkansas and very involved in his church there. This story has a wonderful future!

The second young man I want to brag about has also become a son to me. His name is Quentin Heard. My daughter, Melanie, met him at a church function at college. I clearly remember her telling me she couldn't wait for me to meet him because he was such a leader. I could tell by the way she talked about him that Quentin must be special. She invited him to the lake house with several other kids, and it didn't take long for me to see there was something different about Quentin.

Quentin is the type of person who is extremely teach-able. When he came to the lake, we took several kids in the boat to learn to ski. Many tried multiple times and just couldn't get up. When Quentin's turn came,

I told him to bend his knees, keep his skis in front of him, don't let go of the rope, and that the boat will pull him up. He took all of that literally. He was under water for what seemed like thirty seconds, doing everything I told him- including not letting go of the rope! He was so determined to get this right. When he popped up out of the water, the entire boat erupted with applause. Not just because he got up on his first try, but because of his tenacious spirit that would not be denied! Knowing his past makes this more special to me.

Quentin's mother was single and gave birth to Quentin when she was only fourteen years old. Quentin's two other brothers came along later. It was a financial struggle for his mom. Quentin had to grow up quickly because of the things he saw around him. By the time he was fourteen years old, he was acting as the father figure to his two brothers and taking on odd jobs to help his mom pay the bills. He played sports in high school and also worked. When Melanie first met him, he was nineteen years old and rode a bicycle to work every morning at 6:00 a.m. He would work all day and was paying his way through night school at the local junior college. Through all of this, he was still helping his mom. As we got to know his story, we felt the Lord wanted us to help him in some way.

I had recently become involved with Highlands College in Birmingham, serving on its Board of

Directors. This two-year program helps young people who have a calling to do ministry work. Churches all over the country hire these young people because of the training they receive. It is a fantastic way to fulfill what Jesus told us to do when He saw people hurting. We are called to pray that people will go into the harvest field:

> *"Seeing the people, He felt compassion for them, because they were distressed and dispirited like sheep without a shepherd. Then He said to His disciples, 'The harvest is plentiful, but the workers are few. Therefore, beseech the Lord of the harvest to send out workers into His harvest'"* (*Matthew 9:36-38*).

As we learned Quentin's story, Lucy and I again felt that it was no coincidence that he had become friends with our daughter. We prayed about it, and both of us felt that he would be a perfect fit for Highlands College. But it would be a huge step for him because he had such a burden to help his family. We asked him to pray about moving to Birmingham and attending the college. He prayed and felt it was what the Lord wanted him to do with his life. We arranged a full scholarship to pay for his tuition, and today he has been through the program and has a job working in Texas. He will be an absolute success in life because of his attitude and his love for God. All we did was help open a door.

I can get very passionate talking about these two young men because I have seen their lives change dramatically. They would have had great lives even if they hadn't met me, but God chose me to help open some doors for them. Because I was obedient, He continues to bless me so that I can do the same for others.

Luke 16:11 (NIV) says, *"So if you have not been trustworthy in handling worldly wealth, who will trust you with true riches?"* If we take the money that we have been given and use it to help other people, then I believe God looks on that with favor and gives us the true riches, which is eternal life in heaven.

As we take our resources and use them to help others, we are fulfilling the promise that God gave to Abraham several thousand years ago: that through his descendants the families of the earth will be blessed. What an amazing thought it is to realize we are a part of fulfilling this promise!

Are we allowed to enjoy our possessions?

As with the other topics, the answer is clear in the Bible, and we will see several passages regarding this. But first, I'll say that I believe it really boils down to the attitude of our heart. If money and possessions are what we are seeking, then we will never find true happiness in those things. God wants our heart to be focused on Him and His purpose, which is to see the lost people redeemed. When this is our focus, then our enjoyment here on earth is not only possible, but is God's desire for us. As a father loves his children, so God loves us and wants what is best for us.

I have heard the saying many times that God doesn't care if we have things, but He does care if things have us. In other words, we cannot let the things in our lives be too important. In *The Blessed Life*, Robert Morris says, "God doesn't want us to catch the vision of getting. He wants us to catch the vision of giving." As we are continually looking around us for people we can help, we will see opportunities to be a blessing to others. And as we practice this, God will open the door for more blessings to come our way, so we can continue to give.

In the course of living our life and being a blessing to others, we will experience many blessings in return. Remember what Luke says: *"Give, and it will be given to you. Good measure, pressed down, running over, will be put into your lap. For with the measure you use it will be measured back to you"* (*Luke 6:38 ESV*). God is saying here that we receive back with the same measure that we give, so if we give with a thimble, we receive back with a thimble. If we give with a bucket, we receive back with a bucket. We determine the amount we get back!

I have found this to be true in my life. I did not set out to be financially successful, but I was always sensitive to helping people above and beyond my tithing to the church. I have found that, as I have done this, I have received more in return so that I can continually give to others and be a bigger blessing. I firmly believe that if I decided to stop being a blessing to others when I am presented with a need and begin to hoard my possessions, then God would simply find someone else to pour His blessings through.

We have all heard it said that we cannot out-give God, so how should we respond with our money when we receive back from Him? God gives us wisdom in how to handle our possessions when we are blessed financially.

Luke tells a story of a man who stopped Jesus in a crowd and told Him to tell the man's brother to divide the inheritance with him. Jesus responded, *"Beware, and be on your guard against every form of greed; for not even when one has an abundance does his life consist of his possessions."* Jesus went on to tell them a parable:

> *"The land of a rich man was very productive. And he began reasoning to himself, saying, 'What shall I do, since I*

have no place to store my crops?' Then he said, 'This is what I will do: I will tear down my barns and build larger ones, and there I will store all my grain and my goods. And I will say to my soul, "Soul, you have many goods laid up for many years to come; take your ease, eat, drink and be merry."' But God said to him, 'You fool! This very night your soul is required of you; and now who will own what you have prepared?' So is the man who stores up treasure for himself, and is not rich toward God" (Luke 12:15-21).

This parable highlights some important points. Jesus said the man in the story was a fool for not knowing what to do with his wealth. The man was very wealthy, but instead of looking for ways to bless others with his wealth, he was thinking of how he could store it. I certainly don't believe this is saying not to save and invest in the future, but the man seemed more concerned with his own desires than those of others.

Jesus also said that instead of storing up treasures for himself, the man needed to be rich toward God. Again, the focus should be away from us and our needs; rather, it should be focused on others and how we can please God.

Choosing to sit back and relax without considering how to help the kingdom does not please God, even when—and perhaps especially when—one has accumulated a large amount of money. I think of this when I am asked what my personal exit strategy is with my business. Will I sell it and cash out? If so, my life could be easy for many years. But this passage shows me I would not be pleasing God if I did so. I see no mention in the Bible for retiring to an easy life. As a matter of fact, the only place I can see that mentions retirement is for the Levitical priests in the Old Testament. Instead of retiring to an easier life, I want to constantly be challenging myself to get more out of this life, so I can give more back.

I have been very fortunate to meet John Maxwell several times in the last few years, and he is someone I want to emulate. At seventy years old, he is probably the most intentional person I know. He pushes himself with an extremely busy schedule, so he can have the greatest impact on others and add value to them. He still writes books each year that are impacting millions of people around the world. He could easily slow down and enjoy a more relaxed life, but his heart is to please God so that he can receive the more important rewards that await in heaven. He has certainly inspired me to do the same.

Does all this mean we are not allowed to enjoy ourselves with a game of golf, or hunting, or sporting events, or any other fun events we have come to enjoy? Absolutely not! As a matter of fact, God sincerely does want us to enjoy our lives. I have always felt that if Christians weren't able to show the world that we can have fun, then how are we ever going to reach them and attract them to our way of living? I believe God has given us the tools and the abilities to do just that. The apostle Paul told Timothy, *"Command those who are rich in this present age not to be haughty, nor to trust in uncertain riches but in the living God, who gives us richly all things to enjoy" (1 Timothy 6:17)*. It looks to me like Paul was instructing Timothy to tell the people with financial means that it was fine to enjoy their wealth, so long as they did not put their trust in that wealth.

In *How to be Rich*, Andy Stanley puts it like this:

> "If you are rich in this life, don't be arrogant and please don't place your hope in wealth. It's so uncertain. Instead, place your hope in God who richly provides you with everything for your enjoyment. Do good! Be rich in good deeds! Be generous and willing to share. When you do, you lay up a treasure for yourself that serves as a firm foundation in the coming age. And that's not all. Selfless generosity allows you to take hold of life as it was meant to be lived."

Ecclesiastes also contains a great verse showing that God wants us to enjoy our lives. Solomon, the wisest man to have ever lived, wrote three books of the Old Testament as well as a couple of the Psalms. According to the Bible, people came from all over the world just to hear his wisdom. He stated, *"Furthermore, as for every man to whom God has given riches and wealth, He has also empowered him to eat from them and to receive his reward and rejoice in his labor; this is the gift of God" (Ecclesiastes 5:19)*.

Solomon is saying that it is a gift from God for us to be able to enjoy the results from our labors. We must not get hung up on living a strict pious life that attracts nobody. But on the flip side, we cannot let our hearts chase wealth and fame because that will bring destruction. As with everything in life, it simply requires balance.

If you are conflicted over whether doing something that brings you enjoyment is the right thing to do, simply ask God for wisdom. The Bible says that God gives wisdom freely to anyone who asks Him.

An area of my life that needed change was vacations-or, more precisely, the lack thereof. My wife and I were married for fourteen years when we took our first week off together. Our twins were four years old. I had felt that, because I was self-employed, I must always stay close to the business and be there for all the many problems that would inevitably arise if I left. However, when we went out west for a family reunion, I had a life-changing event: I realized that everything was fine while I was gone! And more importantly, I felt more relaxed and energized when I returned to work.

I told Lucy after that trip that I would commit to taking at least one vacation every year, and we have kept that commitment. I have now visited all fifty states and been able to see many beautiful parts of the country that I never would have seen had I not made that commitment. The point is that God is pleased with us being able to enjoy ourselves, so long as there is balance in our lives.

There is a peace in the ability to enjoy God's blessings. Just remember that there is also an enemy out there who would love to distract you and keep you from God's best for your life. As wealth increases in your life, just keep this perspective: God has given it to you to enjoy so long as you are giving to others and remembering where it all comes from. Remember that Deuteronomy tells us that it is God who gives us the power to make wealth.

My current pastor, Chris Hodges, once said, "If the enemy can't destroy you with bad things, he will distract you with good things to keep you from the best things." Don't let the enemy have the pleasure of changing your focus in life.

Sometimes, giving is not just about wealth. There are other ways we can give of ourselves.

Is giving limited to our money?

Before you conclude that you just don't have any extra money to give away and just move on to the next chapter, let's see what other ways the Bible says you can give to others.

Living in the South, you see poverty in many areas. But oftentimes, the ones who have little are the greatest givers. Remember when Jesus saw the poor lady who put the single coin in the offering? He said she gave more than the others because she gave what she couldn't afford. But He also said that, *"If anyone gives even a cup of cold water to one of these little ones who is my disciple, truly I tell you, that person will certainly not lose their reward" (Matthew 10:42)*. Jesus made it clear to us that even giving something of little significance does not go unnoticed by God.

This verse reminds me of my late mother-in-law, Lois Cannon. She divorced and moved to the South in the late 1960's. She had six children and was a school teacher who didn't make much money, but she taught invaluable lessons to them that are being passed on to grandchildren and now great-grandchildren. Lois could not ignore someone who was doing without. She knew the children in the school who could not afford lunch and had to receive lunch vouchers. Even though she was living with nothing, she would always find ways to help these families. Her small salary kept her from being able to do much, but at Thanksgiving she would cook a meal and then load up the kids in the car and take it to a family who couldn't afford a meal. My wife talks about the impact this had on them because they didn't have money to buy clothes, yet they were giving to others.

To see the impact this had on the children watching would be hard to put in words. All six of these kids could have played the "victim card" and just blamed their parents for divorcing and making life so difficult on them. But instead, they each paid their own way through college through jobs and whatever loans they could get, and all of them have become contributors to society in meaningful ways. Each of them is always willing to help others because they were taught that, as bad as things seemed financially for them, there were always others who had it worse.

The best fruit that came out of this for me is to see how my wife, Lucy, has passed this compassion on to our girls. Not only can they not just walk by someone who is hurting, but they seem to have a radar that goes up when someone is in the room and is hurting or has a need. When they were in school, Lucy would always ask them who they helped that day. If someone was hurting and they comforted them, that was the discussion topic at dinner. When my daughters write sweet notes to their Mom for her birthday or Mother's Day, they always thank her for teaching them to help others who are less fortunate. This is something that will be passed on to their children as well, and I must thank Lois for imparting this to her children. She is receiving amazing rewards in heaven!

Looking for ways to make a difference in the lives of others is something we, as Christians, should do. In *True Measure of a Man*, Richard E. Simmons III points out that "We are seldom taught that the key to experiencing a meaningful life is to make a difference in the lives of others." As we read the Bible, we can see many examples about how we are supposed to do good works. Both Paul, writing to the Ephesian churches, and James, the brother of Jesus, talked about how we were put in this world to do good works.

Paul said that we were created for good works. *"For we are His workmanship, created in Christ Jesus for good works, which God prepared beforehand, that we should walk in them" (Ephesians 2:10)*. None of us can say that we are not givers just because we have no money to give. We can all give of our time and talent to do good works to help our fellow man who is in need.

To further emphasize how our good deeds are to work in conjunction with our faith, we can turn to James. He told us that we cannot have faith alone, but that our faith becomes evident by the things that we do. Studying the book of James is a great way to understand how we should live our lives. He explained the difference in faith and works and that the two cannot be separated, but they must work together.

Here is what James said:

> *"What use is it, my brethren, if someone says he has faith but he has no works? Can that faith save him? If a brother or sister is without clothing and in need of daily food, and one of you says to them, 'Go in peace, be warmed and be filled,' and yet you do not give them what is necessary for their body, what use is that? Even so faith, if it has no works, is dead, being by itself. But someone may well say, 'You have faith and I have works; show me your faith without the works, and I will show you my faith by my works'"* (James 2:14-18).

When you think about this, you can see how faith and work correspond together. We know we are saved by believing what Jesus did for us on the cross. There is no other way to get to God. We must accept His sacrifice for our sins. But once we have accepted that and embark on living a Christian life, then our faith is manifested by the deeds that we do. Caring for the needy and helping those around us can have amazing results. The world is watching us, and we show that we have faith in God by meeting the needs of others, and not just focusing on our own needs:

> *"This service that you perform is not only supplying the needs of the Lord's people, but is also overflowing in many expressions of thanks to God. Because of the service by which you have proved yourselves, others will praise God for the obedience that accompanies your confession of the gospel of Christ, and for your generosity in sharing with them and with everyone else" (2 Corinthians 9:12-13 NIV).*

Paul is saying that, when we share with others and meet needs, people will praise God because our faith is working in our good deeds toward others. This ties in directly to what James was saying in his passage.

In his book *The Purpose Driven Life*, Rick Warren puts it in modern terms: "While many best-selling books offer advice on how to get the most out of life, that's not the reason God made you. You were created to add to life on earth, not just take from it. God wants you to give something back. The Bible says God has created us for a *life of good deeds* which he has already prepared for us to do" (emphasis mine).

God has created us for this life of good deeds. Jesus exhorted us not to hide the light that is within us, but rather to *"let your light shine before men in such a way that they may see your good works, and glorify your Father who is in heaven" (Matthew 5:16)*.

Doing good deeds and giving to others does not always have to involve money. It is often said that the greatest gift you can give someone is your time. I believe this is so true, especially with children. But it is true with others as well. My wife and I both lost our moms within the past two years. They both lived full lives into their late eighties, but their latter years were filled with loneliness and physical ailments that come with old age. Seeing this up close with them and also with my father a few years earlier makes it clear to me why the Bible says often that we are to visit the widows. They are lonely, but they just want someone to love them and give them some time. For weeks, my wife drove for two hours each way- four hours a day- just to sit with her mom for a few minutes and then return home, because her mom couldn't handle long visits. I know this meant the world to Lucy's mom, but it was never easy or convenient. Lucy did it because she loved her mom.

Jesus said that none of these acts of kindness will go unnoticed, and that rewards are being stored in heaven by those who do them. I also believe my wife will receive the reward of having her girls spend time with her when she is elderly because the Bible is clear that we reap what we sow.

Another good example of this in my life is when I lost my younger brother, David, to a heart attack when he was too young to die. Two of my best friends, William Edwards, and Wayne Dunavant, came and spent time with me when they knew I was hurting.

William, my college buddy who relentlessly shared Jesus with me until I became a Christian, took off work and came from out-of-state to spend time with me. After the funeral, we went back to my house and I told him he should go home so he could get back to work. He told me he wasn't leaving me alone for a couple of days, and that work would be there when he got back. He knew as well as anyone how close I was to David, and just wanted to be with me in my time of grief.

Likewise, Wayne is one of the most giving people I know. He is like the modern Good Samaritan, because he always stops and helps people. When he heard that David had passed away, he was out of town in Texas and called me as soon as he heard the news. He wanted to fly home to be with me during the funeral, but I told him not to because it was not necessary to inconvenience himself like that. He came home as planned a few days after the funeral and called me on the phone. Instead of asking if he could come over, he asked me where I was and said he was coming to see me. He came to my house and just sat with me all afternoon, just to talk and keep my mind off David.

I share these two stories because it is something I will never forget. We will always remember who was there during the toughest times in our lives. I want to make sure I am always conscious of the hurts and needs of the people around me because sometimes just being sensitive to other people can make an eternal difference in their life. And that is what God wants us to seek. We are His body doing His work on this earth. And we show the world that we are His disciples by the way we love others. As I have heard my Pastor, Chris Hodges, say, "God doesn't want to just give *to* you, He wants to give *through* you."

Nothing is as fulfilling as when we are helping other people. I believe this is how God designed us, to be fulfilled by helping others. My good friend, Lee Domingue, says it this way in his book *Pearls of the King*: "When someone is in real need and you have the power to help them, always err on the side of generosity. This is not only a biblical truth, but also a way to keep greed in check."

We must constantly remind ourselves that our life on earth is limited by a specific number of days and that only God knows the number. My pastor often says that our ultimate purpose in life is to make a difference in others. I believe this concept aligns well with these comments on giving, because if you don't feel you have any money to give, you can begin by giving your time to help make a difference to others. As you make this a habit, God will use you in progressively bigger ways.

Giving to others also helps us keep our eyes off our own problems until they just seem to work out. In *The Purpose Driven Life*, Rick Warren says, "The old comparison between the Sea of Galilee and the Dead Sea is still true. Galilee is a lake full of life because it takes in water but also gives it out. In contrast, nothing lives in the Dead Sea because, with no outflow, the lake has stagnated. Rick is saying that our life is more fulfilled and more vibrant when we are giving to others.

We receive rewards on this earth when we give. The Bible is very clear on this, and my own life bears it out. But I don't believe that should be our primary motivation. The motivation needs to be centered on eternity and the rewards that are waiting us there as we do the good works that God has called us to do. These good deeds are all around us every day.

We all know from Scripture that a judgment is coming when Jesus will separate the believers from the unbelievers. Did you know that there is another judgment coming that will reward you according to your deeds? Remember, the deeds do not get us into heaven. Only believing on Christ's sacrifice for our sins will get us to heaven. But there are many references to this second judgment that comes to the believers once they get to heaven that will determine the rewards they have for eternity. These rewards are based on the good deeds done for others.

Paul was speaking to the church in Corinth when he said, *"For we must all appear before the judgment seat of Christ, so that each of us may receive what is due us for the things done while in the body, whether good or bad" (2 Corinthians 5:10 NIV)*. This was not said to a group of unbelievers, but to the church, so they would understand that God's plan is not for us to just live a cozy life on earth, but to look to the needs of others.

Paul further explained this in his letter to the church in Ephesus when he said, *"Be very careful, then, how you live - not as unwise but as wise, making the most of every opportunity, because the days are evil" (Ephesians 5:15-16 NIV)*. This sounds very similar to what Moses said in the Psalms. Psalm 90 was the only Psalm attributed to Moses as the author. In it, he asked God to *"Teach us to number our days, that we may gain a heart of wisdom" (Psalm 90:12 NIV)*. Both Paul and

Moses, writing hundreds of years apart, are telling us to spend our time wisely. One of the best ways I believe we can do that is to be engaged in helping others. Or to put it another way, John Maxwell says in *Your Road Map for Success,* "Success is knowing your purpose in life, growing to reach your maximum potential, and sowing seeds that benefit others."

In another letter, Paul mentioned the rewards that come with our good works. When something is mentioned several times in the Bible, I believe God wants it to get our attention. With regard to the judgment, Paul said, *"Their work will be shown for what it is, because the Day will bring it to light. It will be revealed with fire, and the fire will test the quality of each person's work. If what has been built survives, the builder will receive a reward" (1 Corinthians 3:13-14 NIV).* Jesus also mentioned this event when He said, *"For the Son of Man is going to come in his Father's glory with his angels, and then He will reward each person according to what they have done" (Matthew 16:27 NIV).*

During the holidays at the end of the year, Church of the Highlands gives out "random acts of kindness" cards. These cards are the size of a business card, so they fit easily in a wallet or purse. People who want to participate are encouraged to find someone they can bless, and then do something nice for them and leave the card. The random acts include paying for meals in a drive-through for the person behind you, leaving large tips at restaurants, paying for someone's groceries at the store, and on and on. The card simply says, "Something extra to show that God loves you." There are literally thousands of these that go out each year in our cities, blessing people around us. The impact this makes is amazing. People call into our church and tell us how they were having a bad day, or going through a dark time, and this gave them hope. It does make a difference and is a great example of how we can obey what God has called us to do.

Recently I was at a Walmart standing in line waiting to pay. The lady in front of me looked to be a grandmother who was shopping for a child's birthday. She had a few gifts in her basket. When the cashier told her the price, she looked at the toys and started removing a couple of them because it was apparently more than she could afford. I stepped in front of her and paid the bill, so she could get all the toys she had picked. This sweet lady almost started to cry. I don't know her, and she doesn't know me, but the feeling I had that day will not soon be forgotten. I am so thankful that God puts me in those situations. I know that my allowing God to use me in those situations pleases Him, and He continues to bless me so that I can do it again.

In the very last chapter of the Bible, Jesus said, *"Look, I am coming soon! My reward is with me, and I will give to each person according to what they have done"*

(Revelation 22:12). I hope this section has encouraged you to find ways to be a blessing to others.

Commit to creating the habit of giving in your life. The topic of possessions and money is one of the most frequently discussed topics in the Bible for a reason. If handled correctly, it can be used as a tremendous blessing to those around us, and God will make sure we always have enough for every good work. As Margaret Thatcher said, "No one would have remembered the Good Samaritan if he hadn't had money."

Habit Number Five
Confess the Word

"With the fruit of a man's mouth his stomach will be satisfied; he will be satisfied with the product of his lips. Death and life are in the power of the tongue, and those who love it will eat its fruit." (Proverbs 18:20-21)

This habit has radically changed my life. The other habits - studying the Word, hearing and obeying God, fasting, and giving - are all topics you have probably heard in your church over the years. This habit, however, is one that isn't talked about as much, but it can have as large of an impact on your life as the others. I first stumbled upon this as a new Christian reading my Bible. I didn't fully understand it, so I bought books on the subject and studied it because I saw how important it is in our lives.

James said that learning what to say with our mouths can direct our entire lives. So naturally, it is important to understand!

> *"For we all stumble in many ways. If anyone does not stumble in what he says, he is a perfect man, able to bridle the whole body as well. Now if we put the bits into the horses' mouths so that they may obey us, we direct their entire body as well. Behold, the ships also, though they are so great and are driven by strong winds, are still directed by a very small rudder, wherever the inclination of the pilot desires. So also the tongue is a small part of the body, and yet it boasts of great things. Behold, how great a forest is set aflame by such a small fire! And the tongue is a fire, the very world of iniquity; the tongue is set among our members as that which defiles the entire body, and sets on fire the course of our life, and that is set on fire by hell"* (James 3:2-6).

James is saying here that although the tongue is such a small part of our body, it can guide our entire lives if we use it correctly. Unfortunately, it can guide our lives down the wrong path as well. Consider James's example of a rudder. The rudder on a ship is a very small part of the ship; yet it can still direct the ship on the wrong course, ending up in an entirely different destination than where it had planned.

James also says that if a man can learn to bridle his tongue, he can bridle his whole body as well. This is a discipline that can be learned and can have a significant impact on your future. *Proverbs 16:23* proves this, saying, *"The heart of the wise teaches his mouth."* The writer wouldn't have said it if it weren't possible!

For several years, I had horses at my house. My family enjoyed riding them and this created many happy memories for all of us. It was amazing to me how such a small bit in their mouths could get them to do what you wanted. The bit has a ring on both sides of the outside of the horse's mouth that is attached to the reins. When you barely pull the reins, the small curved bit in their mouth presses on the roof of their mouth, making them respond to what you want them to do. You barely need to pull on the rein for them to change direction. The bit only weighs a few ounces, yet it directs a horse weighing several hundred pounds with just a simple pressure.

In the same way, James says that learning how to use our mouth will direct the path for our lives as well. We can determine where we will end up by simply learning how to speak properly. This was an amazing revelation to me, and should be to you, because there are no qualifiers required- like where you were born, how much money you have, or who your parents were. The Bible simply says that you can establish the direction and outcome of your life by learning how to use what you say correctly.

Most of the book of Proverbs was written by King Solomon, who was the wisest man to have ever lived. Because he asked God for wisdom in dealing with the people instead of riches and long life, God gave him wisdom as well as riches. Solomon wrote the Proverbs so that we could read them and gain more wisdom in our lives. He spoke in several places about the importance of what we say. One example comes from Proverbs: *"With the fruit of a man's mouth his stomach will be satisfied; he will be satisfied with the product of his lips. Death and life are in the power of the tongue, and those who love it will eat its fruit"* (Proverbs 18:20-21). He also wrote, *"from the fruit of a man's mouth he enjoys good"* (Proverbs 13:2).

Solomon is telling us that words that we speak are so important that even life and death are in our words. The New Testament echoes this when Paul says that we are saved with the confession of our mouth. *"For it is with your heart that you believe and are justified, and it is with your mouth that you profess your faith and are saved"* (Romans 10:10 NIV). Likewise, Jesus said, *"By your words you will be justified or condemned"* *(Matthew 12:37)*.

Jesus also said that *"Every careless word that men shall speak, they shall render account for it in the day of judgment"* *(Matthew 12:36)*. We can clearly see that the words we speak are important. Learning to speak the right words will have an impact not only on this present life, but also on eternity.

The old saying that "sticks and stones may break my bones, but words will never hurt me" is simply not true. It was perhaps started by a loving parent who was trying to encourage their child to not take offense at hurtful words. The truth, however, is that words do hurt us and can have an impact on our lives if we don't know how to correct them. Everyone can stop and think of a teacher, a coach, or even a parent, who said something years ago that still hurts.

Learn and understand how to correct this in your life. We can all think back to hurtful words spoken over us that have had an impact, good or bad. The reality is that you can determine what words you are going to believe, and I will explain how this can change your thinking about who you are.

What we say is important. Did you know that God created the entire world with His spoken word? The third verse of the Bible says, *"Then God said, 'Let there be light,' and there was light"* *(Genesis 1:3)*. This same phrase is used each time something was created. In other words, God spoke creation into existence with His words.

After God had created everything on the earth, including the waters, the fish in them, the plants and trees, the animals, and the stars in the sky, He said, *"Let Us make man in Our image, according to Our likeness" (Genesis 1:26)*. After God created everything with His spoken word, He then created us in His image. This means that, like God, our spoken word also has power. As you read this and compare it to the other verses in Proverbs and James, you can see that God has placed an emphasis on learning how to control what we say.

We receive what we speak with our mouth and then believe with faith.

God gave us the same power to speak things into existence, if we have faith. Jesus said, *"Truly I say to you, whoever says to this mountain, be taken up and cast into the sea, and does not doubt in his heart, but believes that what he <u>says</u> is going to happen, it shall be granted him" (Mark 11:23*, emphasis mine*)*. If we speak something and believe it with faith, then it will be done for us. To illustrate this powerful lesson, Jesus shared it right after a tree withered because He spoke to it that it would not bear fruit again. He did this to show His disciples the importance of learning how to speak.

If the words we speak are so important, then what exactly should we speak?

What should we speak?

Words are important. I received the following revelation on this subject many years ago. We know that we must have faith to please God. I believe this is because we must believe in Him when we cannot see Him. The Bible says it this way: *"And without faith it is impossible to please Him, for he who comes to God must believe that He is, and that He is a rewarder of those who seek Him" (Hebrews 11:6).* If we must have faith to believe in God, where does this faith come from? The Bible always has the answer: we get our faith from hearing the word of Christ. *"Faith comes from hearing, and hearing by the word of Christ" (Romans 10:17).* If you put these two verses together, you see as I did that hearing God's Word will increase our faith, which we need to please God.

I submit to you that one of the most vital things you can do as a Christian is to learn to confess Scriptures out loud. Gather some Scriptures for building faith, boldness, victory over sin, healing, victory over finances, and any other topic that matters to you. Write these down and confess them regularly. I have been doing this for over 30 years and am amazed at how God will bring them to my mind when I need them during the day.

You can download the Scriptures that I have been using for many years now at 5habitsforanabundantchristianlife.com.

Use this as a guide, or just gather some that are important to you and start confessing them. It will make a difference in your life.

Remember how Jesus told His disciples that it was going to be better when He left them because He would send them the Holy Spirit? One of the advantages of the Holy Spirit is that He is always present to remind us of the words of Jesus. *"But the Helper, the Holy Spirit, whom the Father will send in My name, He will teach you all things, and bring to your remembrance all that I said to you" (John 14:26)*. By not only reading the Word, but sowing it deep into our heart, we allow the Holy Spirit to bring it up when we need it. Get the Word deep in your heart, for *"the mouth speaks out of that which fills the heart" (Matthew 12:34)*.

I read a small book in college that helped open my eyes on this subject. It was *The Tongue - A Creative Force* by Charles Capps, and it said, "The secret to having faith is to continually say what God said." By speaking what the Word says, we can increase our faith. To operate in faith, we must learn to speak with faith. Paul said, *"But having the same spirit of faith, according to what is written, 'I believe, therefore I spoke,' we also believe, therefore also we speak" (2 Corinthians 4:13).*

The young man I spoke about in the last chapter, Quentin, made a profound statement when we were hosting a small group at our house. This was a group of college students who were always curious as to how we can hear from God and know His will. One time, a student asked, "How do I know the will of God?" and Quentin offered this answer: "Just read the Bible out loud!" Think about this. Does God want you sick? Is it His will that you are sick? The Bible has several verses that speak about this. It says that Jesus *"took our infirmities and carried away our diseases" (Matthew 8:17).* Also, *"by the stripes of Jesus, we were healed" (1 Peter 2:24). Proverbs 4:22* says God's words *"are life to me and health to my whole body."*

If the Bible is to be taken as true, then we must believe these verses mean that God wants us to be free from sickness. Does this mean we are never going to get sick? No, it does not. But what we can do when we are sick is to confess these Scriptures out loud and stand on them, claiming that this is God's will for our health. I don't believe sickness comes from God. But I do believe we can stand in faith and speak what God has already said about us concerning sickness.

An example I love to use for claiming God's promises is a story found in the Old Testament book of Numbers. The children of Israel had seen many miracles while escaping slavery under Pharaoh in Egypt. They ended up wandering in the wilderness because they doubted God. When they finally got to the edge of the Promised Land, which was Canaan, Moses sent twelve spies in to bring back a report to him about what they saw.

Remember, this is the land that God had already said He was going to give to them. They had been hearing about this for years, ever since leaving Egypt. They had seen amazing miracles, including daily food and water. So you would think they were full of faith about this new land they were about to receive!

When Moses chose the twelve men and sent them into the land, they came back and reported that the land was full of milk and honey. They even brought fruit to show Moses how fertile the land was. But ten of the twelve spies chose to focus on the fact that the people living there were very large and reported that they would not be able to overcome them. Only Joshua and Caleb gave a good report that, although the people were large and numerous, God would deliver them into their hands. Joshua and Caleb were simply saying what God had already said — He was going to give them this land. Joshua and Caleb believed that God would do what He had said He would do.

Because of this faith in what God said, Joshua and Caleb were the only men of the spies who were eventually allowed to enter the land. Because the other ten spies had doubted, and convinced the people to also doubt, God was angry with them. He told Moses that they would all wander around for years in the wilderness before entering the land. The men would all die in the wilderness and their sons would inherit the land. Even Moses was only allowed to see the land from a distance as the people were preparing to enter many years later.

After all the years of wandering, God chose Joshua to take Moses's place as leader of the people. Joshua was given the task of conquering all the people and then dividing the land amongst the twelve tribes. All because he had faith that God was able to do what He said He would do!

How does this apply to us today? God has given us His Word and He wants us to believe it. We don't have to doubt that God wants us to be healthy, or to have success in our life; He has already said so in His Word. Our job is to believe what He has said. The best way I have found to do that is to confess the Scriptures out loud. By confessing them and hearing them, our faith is raised.

Remember that God created the whole world with His spoken Word and then created us in His image.

He gave us a blueprint on how we can use words to create life in situations. As Capps tells us in *The Tongue - A Creative Force,* "Words are like little seeds that produce after their kind. Learn to pray according to the Word of God. God's Word will produce after His kind."

I am sure there are people in your life who always seem gloomy, seeing the glass as half-empty instead of half-full. Many people are just looking for problems with their situations. Don't be one of those people! Besides being unpleasant company, these people often draw negative things to them. On the other hand, we can speak about good things and see how positive our life becomes. As the Bible puts it, *"Finally, brothers and sisters, whatever is true, whatever is noble, whatever is right, whatever is pure, whatever is lovely, whatever is admirable--if anything is excellent or praiseworthy--think about such things" (Philippians 4:8 NIV).*

Learning to control what we say can have dramatic influence on our future. It can also determine to a large extent who we become. "Perhaps the most powerful words in your vocabulary are the words you say to yourself and believe," Brian Tracy suggests in *Million Dollar Habits.* Learn to speak what you want in life, and where you want to be.

Benefits of Confessing the Word

A great benefit of doing this is that it will build our faith to do greater things.

❖ Confessing the Word will build your faith

Have you ever heard the statement that you will never outgrow your self-image? I heard this as a young man and decided I would work on my self-image. Anyone can improve their self-image, no matter where they are or what they have been through.

For anyone to accomplish great things in life, they have to first believe they can do it. Henry Ford was quoted as saying, "If you think you can, or think you can't, either way you are right." This is from a man who revolutionized manufacturing in our country, and the world. He kept pushing his engineers to do things that seemed impossible. For example, he told them to design an engine with cylinders that run off the crankshaft in a "V" pattern. This had been proven to work before, but never in a production environment. They worked for months on this and said it was impossible. He did not give up, but instead continued to focus on this as he believed it would make a more efficient engine. Because of his relentless belief, the engineers perfected this to the point that it is still the most popular design for engines almost one hundred years later. Henry Ford believed something impossible could be done, and he went and made it happen!

Yet before we can get to the point of performing at a high level, we must picture ourselves performing at that high level. A great doctor friend of mine, Don Thomas, used to say, "If you don't see it before you see it, you'll never see it." Sounds funny, but it is true. Brian Tracy puts it like this in *Million Dollar Habits*: "The way you see yourself on the inside largely determines how you perform on the outside." If you read about great athletes who achieved great things, they will almost always say that they saw themselves doing what they eventually did. It is like the little boy taking the last shot at a basketball game. He has practiced that scene over and over in his head and always pictured the ball going into the hoop.

When we are young children, we think we can do just about anything. But as we go to school and get around others, our dreams and goals can be changed. We begin to doubt. We begin to limit ourselves by what others think of us. Many times, a coach, or a teacher, or a parent can tell us we can't do something, and we begin to believe them. Or like Lucy said to Charlie Brown in *Peanuts* by Charles Schulz, "You're in the shadow of your own goalpost! You are a missed goal! You are three putts on the 18th green! You are a 7 - 10 split in the 10th frame... You are a missed free throw, a shank 9 iron and a called third strike! Do you understand? Have I made myself clear?" It is always our decision whether to choose to believe the negative thing that has been said about us.

On the other hand, there are coaches, parents, and teachers who believe in us and tell us we can do great things. These are the ones we should listen to and believe. We do get to decide which side we listen to, and the results can be significant.

We can all think of people who have spoken good words over us and positively impacted our lives. The first person who had this impact on me was my older brother, Derek. When I was fourteen and he was twenty-one, he started letting me tag along with him and do fun things. He taught me to ride motorcycles, ride horses, shoot guns, and other typical guy things. Like all kids that age, I was trying to fit in at school. But once Derek started letting me tag along, it just didn't matter to me what the kids my age thought, because I had an older brother who thought I was cool.

Because of the impact this had on my confidence, I am very intentional about helping others believe in themselves. Many times, this is all they need to move forward in their lives. "Believing in people before they have proved themselves is the key to motivating people to reach their potential," John Maxwell explains in *Relationships 101*.

Someone else who had an early impact on me was a man who lived in my neighborhood. I was always looking for ways to earn money doing odd jobs, like cutting grass, delivering newspapers, etc. In our neighborhood, you had to carry your trash cans to the curb at the road so that the garbage men could come by and empty them. I went to my neighbors and told them that, for two dollars per month, I would come by each Thursday night and carry their trash cans to the street. It certainly wasn't much money for the work involved, but it seemed like a lot to me at the time. When I would go collect my money each month, this one man kept telling me that I was going to be successful in life. His simple encouragement to me was something that I chose to believe. It is funny how we can remember such seemingly small events.

It has been said that we become who the important people in our lives think we are. Unfortunately, this works also to our detriment, when someone we respect belittles us in front of other people or says that we aren't good enough. If you have suffered from this, how can it be changed?

I chose to change my situation by reading positive books, hanging out with people who believed in me, and learning to confess who God said I was.

I started the habit of reading good books when I was in my mid-twenties, because I wanted desperately to learn from others what it took to succeed in life. I came across this quote by Charlie Tremendous Jones: "You will be in five years where you are today except for the people you meet and the books you read." I felt that this was within my control, so I started reading helpful books and seeking relationships with people who believed in me and could build me up.

I also read this quote by Shad Helmstetter from his book *What to Say When You Talk to Yourself*: "You will become what you think about most; your success or failure in anything, large or small, will depend on your programming – what you accept from others, and what you say when you talk to yourself."

I truly believe that we can program our brains to believe we can achieve great things. I am living proof that this works. I did not start out with a good self-image. During high school and the first four years of college, I didn't believe I was really headed anywhere successful. I was just drifting in life and doing things that were detrimental to my future. When I became a Christian, I had a lot of baggage from the things I had done. I felt the devil was constantly reminding me of all my mistakes and I wasn't convinced that I deserved God's love.

This changed for me when I started reading my Bible and seeing all the promises that God gives. I would sit in the library every day and write down verses that were speaking directly to me, verses that told me who I was in Christ, that God loved me, and that *"greater was He that was in me, than he that was in the world"* (1 John 4:4). I started to see that I *"could do all things through Christ who strengthened me"* (Philippians 4:13). Because I wanted to believe these truths about myself, I started confessing them out loud as if they were written just for me.

I would go out to a park several mornings per week and read these verses out loud. I confessed them as if I had already received what they were saying. I still confess verses regularly to this day. It takes about twenty minutes, and I can almost quote every verse in my list. I cannot tell you the impact this has had on my life.

When I started to see in the Bible what my heavenly Father thought of me, it was hard for me to believe I deserved this love because I was not close to my dad (mostly by my own rebellion). By confessing these verses, I began to have the faith that they were true about me. Because I have been doing this now for over three decades, I am convinced of my Father's love and acceptance. I also have faith I can do great things, because God said I can.

Another benefit of confessing Scriptures is that it can help us overcome temptations.

❖ Confessing the Word will help with temptations

When Jesus was about to begin His ministry at thirty years old, He went out into the wilderness and fasted for forty days. He was preparing Himself for what was ahead. During these forty days, the devil came to Him three times and tempted Him. Each time the devil tempted Jesus, Jesus answered by quoting the Old Testament book of Deuteronomy. He began each response with the words "It is written..." The final time, the devil fled from Him and angels came and ministered to Him.

I believe every word is in the Bible for a reason. If God thought something was so important that He put it in there three times, then maybe I should pay attention to what He is saying! This is a great pattern for us to follow in our lives when the devil is tempting us with sin. If he came and tempted Jesus, we can be sure he will come and tempt us. If we want to follow the example that Jesus set for us, then we need to study the Scriptures and know verses that will help when we are tempted.

One of the best verses that I have used over the years is, *"No temptation has overtaken you but such as is common to man; and God is faithful, who will not allow you to be tempted beyond what you are able, but with the temptation will provide the way of escape also, so that you will be able to endure it"* (1 Corinthians 10:13). This verse has helped me many times when I have felt bombarded by the devil. Often it just starts with a bad thought that I have to eradicate. I have prepared myself by making this verse personal to me. In other words, I replace 'no temptation has overtaken you' with 'no temptation has overtaken me'. I have quoted this many times over the years when I needed strength to overcome something, usually unhealthy thoughts.

The Bible says, *"and we are taking every thought captive to the obedience of Christ"* (2 Corinthians 10:5). Sin usually starts with a thought, so we must take those thoughts captive and rebuke them. James told us to *"resist the devil and he will flee from you"* (James 4:7).

If we are going to live a victorious and abundant Christian life, we must learn to overcome the temptations that come our way. The Bible says that our sins separate us from God, yet He hears and answers the prayers of the righteous. This doesn't mean we are to be perfect (since it's impossible anyways). But if there is sin in our life that we have not handled, learning to confess Scripture can help.

Another thought I want to mention before moving on is that the devil does not like you to use the name of Jesus. If you are ever in a situation where your thoughts are not pure, or you feel bombarded by temptation, just say the name of Jesus out loud.

Having worship music close by is also always good. My wife loves to play worship music in our house, and I can say that there is a difference in the environment because of this.

Everyone either has a problem they are facing, or will have one, so knowing how to overcome them when they come will help.

❖ Proper confession will help overcome problems

If there is a situation in our lives that we need God to show up in, several examples in the Bible show us how God responds. When Daniel had fasted for twenty-one days because he wanted to understand a vision that God had given him, an angel appeared to him. The angel told him that God had heard his request the first day he had spoken it and the angel was coming *"in response to his words" (Daniel 10:12)*. This angel explained how answers sometimes are held up because there is a battle going on in the spiritual realm. This allows us to understand how prayers get answered and how we should not give up when asking.

Because all Christians will experience times in their lives when they need an answer from God that is important to them, I am including some verses that will build your faith and comfort you when you are waiting on God. God tells us that if we fear Him and are doing His will, He hears us. *"We know that God does not hear sinners; but if anyone is God-fearing and does His will, He hears him"* (John 9:31).

Not only does He hear us, but if we ask according to His will, He gives us what we ask. *"This is the confidence we have in approaching God: that if we ask anything according to his will, he hears us. And if we know that he hears us--whatever we ask--we know that we have what we asked of him"* (1 John 5:14-15 NIV). The way to know His will is to see if it lines up with what He says in His Word. You don't have to ask if God wants you healed from sickness. The Bible already says He does. Just claim what He has already said about it and believe that you are already healed. He said that Jesus *"took our infirmities and carried away our diseases"* (Matthew 8:17).

Just like Joshua and Caleb, confess what God has already said and then believe that He can, and will, do it. *"And being fully assured that what God had promised, He was able also to perform"* (Romans 4:21).

We must also make sure we are asking with the right motives. *"You covet but you cannot get what you want, so you quarrel and fight. You do not have because you do not ask God. When you ask, you do not receive, because you ask with wrong motives, that you may spend what you get on your pleasures"* (James 4:2-3 NIV). The way to know if our motives are pure is simply to see if they line up with the Bible. If they do, then we can have confidence that we will have what we ask.

When our motives are pure, and we know they line up with God's Word, then we can pray with boldness. *"Let us then approach God's throne of grace with confidence, so that we may receive mercy and find grace to help us in our time of need" (Hebrews 4:16 NIV)*. God loves us as a Father loves His child, and He wants us to know Him and to have a confidence that, by knowing His will for us, we can confidently ask Him for the needs in our life.

We all know that life is never perfect, and that we will go through times that are hard. This is when we need to be grounded in what the Word says. The hardest challenge in my life came when I had been married for about four years and my wife, Lucy, and I decided it was time to have a baby. We loved children and felt we would be great parents who could raise children to love God. Most of our friends were having children, and the timing seemed right for us.

Lucy got pregnant within a few months, and we were so excited. But a couple of months into the pregnancy, she started having problems. It ended up being a tubal pregnancy that required immediate surgery. This was devastating on us, as we did not understand what was happening. About two years after healing from the surgery, she got pregnant again. Once again, it was a tubal pregnancy that luckily was caught before her tube ruptured, which could have been life-threatening.

We were simply devastated! I cannot explain the pain we both went through during this time. We didn't question God, but we also did not understand why we were going through this. It seemed like nobody else had this problem. Our two mothers had ten children between them, and they couldn't understand. We saw people having children very easily who didn't even seem to want them, and we were desperate for our own.

During these two pregnancies we were living in small towns with limited health care, and the doctors were offering little hope that we could get pregnant. One doctor even told us that he did not know what was wrong with us. Talk about having your hope thwarted! We were beyond disappointed, and we had nobody to turn to. It seemed like no one understood our pain.

I was so desperate because I saw my wife hurting so badly on the inside. I was praying every day and asking God to hear us and answer us. I believed it was His will for us to have children. I turned to the one thing I could think of that could help this situation: to start speaking what I wanted to happen. Instead of doubting that I would have children, I chose to speak that we would have children. I noticed that my hope and faith were increased. For two years, I had a three-inch by five-inch card that I carried in my pocket and confessed several times per day. I had written down a few things that I wanted God to do in our lives. One of the phrases that I was confessing was that "Lucy is pregnant, and God is giving us healthy babies." I did not say "baby," but "babies," because we had lost two babies and I wanted the pain removed from our lives by having two.

During this difficult season we went to a doctor in Birmingham who specialized in problem pregnancies. We both got checked out, and for the first time we had a doctor tell us that there was nothing wrong with either of us and that we would get pregnant again. Finally, our hope was restored! It wasn't long after this that Lucy got pregnant again. Because of the problems in the past, she went to the doctor to make sure that everything was going well. The doctor told her that not only was she pregnant, but that she was having twins!

The first thing I thought about when I heard this was that I had been confessing that, "Lucy is pregnant, and God is giving us healthy *babies*." God showed me that He gave us twins because that is what I had been confessing. I remember telling Lucy that not only was this pregnancy going to be successful, but that the babies would be healthy. I figured that if God answered the first part of my confession, He could also answer the second part.

During the pregnancy, Lucy did everything the doctors told her. She drank water all day long. Typically, twins come early and are premature. We went to classes to prepare us for what may happen if they were born early. Lucy had twin brothers who were born early and had to stay in the hospital several days, so we knew this was possible. But her pregnancy went two weeks past term for twins and they were two of the biggest twins ever born at the hospital: six pounds and ten ounces, and seven pounds and two ounces! They were very healthy and have been nothing short of a tremendous blessing in our lives.

I tell you this very personal story because I know there are others who are experiencing something as painful as this, and don't know where to turn or whom to talk to. I recommend claiming what you desire in this situation as if it has already happened. Remember what Jesus said after cursing the fig tree: *"Truly I say to you, whoever says to this mountain, be taken up and cast into the sea, and does not doubt in his heart, but believes that what he says is going to happen, it shall be granted him. Therefore, I say to you, all things for which you pray and ask, believe that you have received them, and they shall be granted you"* (Mark 11:23-24).

Notice here that Jesus told His disciples that if they believed what they said, it would be granted to them. They could even move a mountain! I believe He was telling them- and us- that any mountains in our lives can be moved if we will just learn to speak the right way. We remove the mountains from our lives by speaking directly to them. That is what Jesus did, and since He walked on earth to be an example for us, it follows that we can likewise do the same. Begin to practice this and soon it will become a habit.

Jesus wants us to be productive and bear fruit in our life. This happens as we obey Him and live our lives in accordance with the Word. *"If you abide in Me, and My words abide in you, ask whatever you wish, and it will be done for you. My Father is glorified by this, that you bear much fruit, and so prove to be My disciples"* (John 15:7-8).

Confess what the Bible says about us and who we are in Christ — it can give us the faith and confidence to become all God destined us to become.

6

Summary

"If we could but show the world that being committed to Christ is no tame humdrum, sheltered monotony, but the most thrilling, exciting adventure the human spirit could ever know!" - Dr. James Stewart of Edinburgh

As Christians, we should constantly strive to rise above this lost world. We should be willing to pay a bigger price than the average person because we want to attract others into a real relationship with God. I find that winners want to be around other winners. If we want to attract winners, we must be willing to work first on ourselves. This takes effort that many people are not willing to put forth. Know that the results can be amazing with the impact it has on those around us.

I believe God is always looking for the people who are willing to discipline themselves in their daily life so that they are ready when the opportunity to make a difference comes. In his book *Success, Motivation, and the Scriptures*, William Cook draws the same conclusion:

> "But wouldn't it be just like God... To take one look at the totally yielded Christian who would walk through sufferings and tensions, take another look at a giant task which desperately needed doing, and cast his eye back toward the Christian and write across his life - tested; trustworthy; yielded; motivated from within; ready for the big job!"

Or, as Andy Stanley says in *Visioneering*:

> "Find me a man or woman who has built a great organization and his family is thriving, and I'll show you an opportunity for God to draw big-time attention to himself. That's when outsiders stop to wonder. That's when people are almost forced to conclude that God was involved."

We should desire for people to look at our lives and see that something is different. At that point, we can start relationships and lead them to a Father who loves them.

How do we get to this life that attracts others? We start by finding the things that other people have done to get where we want to be and then duplicate them. Find people who have done things the right way and whose lives show evidence of God's blessings. There are no easy roads. President Teddy Roosevelt said, "There has not yet been a person in our history who led a life of ease whose name is worth remembering." Life is too short to not get as much out of it as we can. Remember that it is easy to live an average life and make little difference. Even a dead fish can float with the current. It takes a strong fish to float against the current. "The hardest struggle of all is to be something different from what the average man is." – Charles M Schwab

We must learn to start where we are, and then make the decision to change. Start to do something today. As Randall Jones advises in *The Richest Man in Town*, "Don't procrastinate because in only two days, tomorrow will be yesterday."

The habits I have discussed in this book can change your life as they have changed mine. But all of them take discipline. I am a very goal-oriented person, maybe even too much at times. (One of my biggest challenges has always been learning how to slow down.) I am certainly better at living with balance than I was as a younger man, but I still feel I have a lot to give. I want my torch to also burn brightly. I believe setting goals has helped me achieve more in life.

Because I am so goal-oriented, I have learned what works for me. I set many goals each year for each area of my life. But I start the year by thinking about the goals that are the most important to me. One of my top goals every year is to know God in a deeper way, so I have 'reading my Bible completely through' as one of my primary goals each year. I look at the important goals and plan my schedule around them first. I read my Bible in the morning before my day starts and the busyness of the day kicks in. H. Jackson Brown, author of *Life's Little Instruction Book* points out, "You pay a price for getting stronger. You pay a price for getting faster. You pay a price for jumping higher. But also, you pay a price for staying just the same." Start by deciding to discipline yourself in one area and see if it makes a change in your life.

Look at what is important to you and decide what you want to accomplish. Remember that everyone who improved themselves started where they were at some point! The individual had to make the decision to change. To change yourself, start with the most important goals first. Look at all your daily tasks as rocks to place in a jar, realizing that the most important tasks are the biggest rocks. Once these rocks are in the jar, the smaller rocks (less important tasks) will be able to fit as well. But, as Richard E. Simmons III tells us in *Wisdom – Life's Greatest Treasure*, "If you don't put the big rocks in first, you'll never get them in at all. The jar is your life. The big rocks are the things that matter most in life, beginning with your relationship with God, your marriage and other important relationships."

Don't settle for an average life. Decide to make a difference and be one of the people whom God blesses and uses in a big way. Early in this book, I shared a verse that has had a significant impact on how I view God. *"For the eyes of the Lord move to and fro throughout the earth that He may strongly support those whose heart is completely His" (2 Chronicles 16:9)*. Let this verse sink into your heart, and see that God is looking for that person who will put Him first in everything and live their life to please Him. You will be amazed if you seek His will and pursue it above all else.

Stephen Covey says in his great book, *The 7 Habits of Highly Effective People*, that we should "begin with the end in mind." This means that we should look at where we are trying to go in life and then figure out what it will take to get there. Then we break it down into daily tasks and do them regularly, and eventually we will have the outcome we were wanting in the beginning.

Realize that, as a father loves his kids, God loves us even more, and wants the very best for us. The abundant life Jesus came and died to give us is worth paying a price to receive. We don't have to physically die, but we must die to self and put Him first if we want to receive all He has in store for us. Make a decision to be one of the few who achieve the abundant life Jesus came to give us. It is there for anyone, but it takes seeking God with all you have.

Remember that God doesn't look at your faults and think He can't use you. If you look at the disciples whom Jesus called- fishermen and tax collectors for instance- you will see they were imperfect men who all had faults. Jesus Himself was a carpenter, which I believe helped Him relate to the crowd of men He would be leading. Don't you think that perhaps Jesus chose these rough men to set an example for us, to show us that it doesn't matter what our background is- just that we plan on moving forward in the right direction? As the old saying goes, "Where you come from doesn't matter as much as where you are going." Decide today to go somewhere where few people have gone. As my good friend, Lee Domingue says in *Pearls of the King*, "if you don't answer God's call, He will call someone else."

God does see greatness and potential in all of us. When He looks at our life, He doesn't see an acorn; He sees an oak tree. It takes time for the acorn to grow into the mighty tree, but God is always wanting us to become the tree and bear fruit. The choice for growth is up to us. As the Irish proverb says, "You've got to do your own growing, no matter how tall your grandfather is." Everything great that has ever been accomplished started with a decision. Make yours today!

I have shared in this book many Bible verses that have changed my thinking and, therefore, my life. But if I had to choose the one verse that has had the most significant impact on where I am today, I would have to say it is Joshua 1:7-8. This is where God gave Joshua instructions for the gigantic task of leading the people into the Promised Land. He told him to meditate day and night on the Scriptures so that he could be careful to do everything that was in them. Then Joshua would be prosperous and successful.

Remember that God was instructing Joshua to meditate on the five books that Moses had left him. It is interesting to me that Jesus was quoting from these when He told the devil to flee from Him. Obviously, Jesus was studying and meditating on these Scriptures, so it makes sense that I should.

As I learned to study and pray on the Scriptures, making it a daily habit in my life, I began to see the other instructions that God had laid out for how I should live. Because I wanted to be obedient, I started viewing what I read as a personal instruction for me- as if God was speaking directly to me through the Bible.

I found through my studies that true success comes when we are obedient to God. I learned to listen, not only when I was reading His Word, but also when I prayed or when I had a decision to make. I always wanted God to lead me so that I could be in the center of His will. By having this simple faith and doing what I believed God wanted me to do, I did things that didn't always make sense in the world's eyes — but I knew that God was always just watching to see if I would obey.

I also learned to form the habits of fasting, giving, and confessing the Word. I believe that fasting and giving have both kept the enemy out of my life and my finances. Learning to confess the Word has built my faith so that, when tough times have come in my life, I have been prepared on how to handle them. I simply stood on what God said to me and about me. I also have noticed that forming these habits and practicing them over time makes them easier to do. In the beginning, forming a habit seems hard; but once you push through with discipline, it becomes second nature. Emerson said, "that which we persist in doing becomes easier – not that the nature of the task has changed, but our ability to do has increased."

Don't feel limited to these five habits. I have formed other habits, like observing the Sabbath once a week. Taking a time of rest is vital for our health and is written about in several places in the Bible, so it must be important. I know this has had a significant impact on my life in the past twenty years. It has helped me be more productive during the six days of the week that I work. I view this like I view tithing. God can make the ninety percent go further when I am obedient to Him; similarly, He can make my six days more productive when I give one day to Him.

I haven't included taking a Sabbath rest as one of the habits simply because I haven't been doing it for over thirty years as I have the other five habits. I wanted to focus on the habits that I feel have had the greatest impact on my life, those that have put me in the position I am in today. I want someone to read this and step out in faith and see that forming these habits can have the impact on their life that it has on mine.

You may read your Bible and have God tell you different things than what He told me. I certainly needed some of these to become habits in my life because I probably had further to go than most. My encouragement to you is to get serious about letting God speak to you through His Word, and then do what He is saying to you personally. If you are reading this and think you just don't have the time to do all these things, start by reading your Bible daily. I impressed this upon my two daughters and it has certainly helped shape their lives. They and their husbands read their Bibles regularly, giving me great encouragement about their futures.

Whatever you do, don't let the enemy place guilt on you because you aren't doing enough. Discouragement does not come from God. He loves us too much; He wants to use us to reach people around us. Make a decision to start something different today that will have a positive impact on your life. Make a decision to become the Christian God wants you to be.

In his thoughtful book *Good to Great in God's Eyes*, Chip Ingram encourages us:

> "Good Christians live the Christian life. They love God, walk in integrity, demonstrate faithfulness to their mates, spend time in the Bible because they want to hear from God, make the effort to discover their spiritual gifts, use those gifts in their local church, give their tithes and offerings, go on mission trips, and help their kids grow up to be godly men and women. They do what God calls them to do, and they serve him well. Great Christians, on the other hand, do all that and then pass it on. You can be a good Christian by obeying God and loving people, but if you haven't poured your life into others, your life ends with a period. Great Christians end with a comma. They live the life of faith in a way that takes God's grace to them and imparts it into the lives of others. They

> multiply themselves again and again and again. Good Christians 'live the life'; great Christians 'leave a legacy.'"

I choose to leave a legacy and have my life end with a comma!

The goal of all of us as Christians should be to get the most out of this life and use the talents God gave us to bless others, thereby storing up treasures in heaven. My ultimate goal is to hear God say, "Well done, good and faithful servant. Enter into My rest." When I eat a steak, I do not want it to be cooked well done. But I certainly want my life to be recorded by God as well done!

I believe that God puts seeds of greatness in all of us, but very few find them or cultivate them to their maximum potential. My prayer is that this book has helped you on your journey.

If you would like to share a story about how one of these habits has affected your life, I would love to hear from you. You may contact me through my website, <u>5habitsforanabundantchristianlife.com</u>.

"I want to be thoroughly used up when I die, for the harder I work the more I live. I rejoice in life for its own sake. Life is no "brief candle" for me. It's a sort of splendid torch which I have got hold of for the moment, and I want to make it burn as brightly as possible before handing it on to future generations." – George Bernard Shaw

My prayer is that this book has encouraged you in some way to diligently pursue the abundant life that Jesus has for each of us willing to seek it. Jesus chose us so that we would go and bear fruit and that our fruit would remain. Let's commit together to making this happen in our lives so our Father is pleased with how we steward the talents He has given us. And then we can make a significant difference in the world around us!

May God's blessings be upon you richly as you continue down your path of life.

Made in the USA
Columbia, SC
29 January 2019